To Bob and S
Hope you enjoy
Best Wishes

Denis

CW00496499

1 Boat 2 Kids 3 Oceans

by Denis Wilkins

ISBN 978-1-5272-3257-0

Produced and printed in Guernsey by Melody Press Printers.

This book was written 27 years ago. It was written as we saw the world then. Something I may have said might not be politically correct in todays standards. No offence to anyone was ever intended.

The Preparation.

In 1986, I purchased a repossessed yacht from the local bank in Guernsey. An Evasion 37 named Yemunja. "what are we going to do with it?' my wife Sadie asked, "I'll take you to the Caribbean" I joked. To my amazement she replied, "That sounds fantastic". The seed was planted and three months later we were on our way!! I set off with my wife and two children Vicky and James aged four and two. That year was one of the happiest years of my life.

After our last voyage the feeling of restlessness gradually crept up on us, until we could not resist the temptation any longer. We jumped in with both feet and decided to buy a bigger Yacht, this time to sail around the world.

Many people have dreams of sailing off into the blue. When the moment actually arrives to do it, it involves a lot of hard work and a certain amount of trepidation creeps in or you could call it downright fear, especially when you have your family on board. It's not quite as irresponsible as it sounds. I spent weeks doing navigation lessons literally at the kitchen table. It took nights of study just to figure out the approximate route I would take so I could order the correct charts. Bearing in mind there were no chart plotters. My navigation was going to be done with a sextant, sight reduction tables and an almanac. We did have a Walker Satnav, but it couldn't be relied on. It was very intermittent as to whether it would work or not.

Food was another big consideration. What food would keep over a long period of time? How to store it correctly? What would be a healthy diet for us, especially our two young children? We stocked up mainly tinned meat, dried fruit and powdered milk.

A comprehensive medical kit had to be compiled. Sadie went to the doctor with a list of medical supplies we might need. He suggested a few other prescriptions such as a strong antibiotic should one of us get appendicitis. A visit to the dentist to get spare tubes of filler should any of our fillings fall out at sea. Another consideration was water. How much could we carry? How long would it last? I had a special canopy made with a small gutter sewn around the edge so we could catch rainwater. I fitted a generator and solar panels to ensure we had enough battery power.

I fitted a Pacific Wind Pilot self steering gear. A good downwind sail plan had to be figured out with the correct Spinnaker pole and fittings.

Schooling had to be worked out by my wife Sadie for the children. We contacted the World Education Service about books we would need for the children's education for three years. We looked into what curriculum the school used in Guernsey, so as not to confuse matters when they joined a 'proper 'school.

We needed spares for anything likely to break or wear out, as in the places we intended to visit, spares would be difficult.

Not least, funding had to be considered and my business was handed over to a manager. We saw an advert in one of the yachting magazines, then a week later we had our tickets booked for Majorca where the yacht "Gringo" was lying. We just fell in love with her. She was a Vagabond 47, built by Blue Water Yachts and looked like she would go through anything. After arranging the necessary bank transfer, we purchased her where she lay, without much thought of how or when we were going to get her back to Guernsey. That turned out to be another saga in our lives. With the extortionate fees of Cala d'or marina we wanted to get her back as soon as possible.

So off we set at the end of March to bring her back to Guernsey. On that trip we encountered some of the worst seas I have had the misfortune to ever experience around Cape St.Vincent. The trip back across the Bay of Biscay turned out to be more eventful than contemplated.

After half way across we ran into thick fog, with only about 200 yards visibility. After staring into the fog for a while you begin to imagine seeing things. But we realised what we were seeing was something like a bad dream. There was a ship wallowing in the centre of Biscay discharging his waste from his tanks. The whole area of sea was covered in a thick brown gunge. This was something we had not expected and I don't think he was expecting us. At first we thought he had a major problem, but soon realised what he was up to. The men that were on deck quickly downed their tools and appeared to run and hide below decks. Suddenly the stationary ship began to move straight for us. I went to follow the rules of the road and pass port to port, but it was obvious he had no intention of doing this. Without doubt, his intention was to run us down. A small yacht is far more manoeuvrable than a huge ship and we managed to take avoiding action, thinking he would then proceed on his way, but to our horror, using his bow thruster and engine, he sharply turned and came at us again and again. I manoeuvred at right angles to avoid him.

This cat and mouse game went on for 20 minutes, even though I repeatedly tried to call him on the radio. It was only when I threatened him to put out an international distress call on the SSB radio did the stupid game stop.

I motored away from him as fast as I could in the opposite direction for at least an hour until I was satisfied I was well away from him. When the fog eventually lifted we were on edge from every ship we saw in case he was coming after us again. We arrived back in Guernsey and reported it to the Harbour Master who said to prove it

would be very difficult. So, we had no choice but to let it drop.
We prepared our boat to the best of our ability encountering more than a few hiccups along the way. If you can get through the trauma of preparing for a long ocean trip, hopefully the rest should be a downhill run. The thing that came out of all the preparation was that I knew my boat intimately.

Heading for the Sunshine

So, here we are again in August 1989 crossing oceans again after only two years of land lubbing. After stretching our finances we set sail for Northern Spain, arriving in La Coruna after four days at sea. The only thing of note along the Spanish and Portuguese Coast was the constant thick fog. We had to navigate either by radar or peer into a blank thick wall. We found we began to imagine things and make out shapes that were not really there. But thank goodness, we saw no more fog after Averio. One nasty experience that we encountered along that coast was a rope around the propeller. I had

Gringo enjoying a downwind sail with my favourite Cruising Chute

to go over the side in a large rolling sea with a knife to get it off. Every time the boat came down on a wave I ended up having a bash on the head from the hull. No matter how I tried I could not avoid it happening. After about ten dives I eventually managed to remove the last piece of rope. I swallowed an awful amount of sea water and came near to the point of exhaustion. I was never more pleased as I pulled the last bit off. The rest of that part of the trip went without further incident and I certainly slept well that night after we anchored up.

All along the Portuguese coast one needs to keep a sharp eye open for fishing pots, bits of rope and polythene bags. Quite often the tuna nets go over 2 miles out to sea from land.

Sadie and the Children in Porto Santo

It was nice to get into the deep blue ocean again on our way to Madeira. A trip that included a fair amount of motoring due to the lack of wind. How lovely it was to see the turtles around us again. At last we began to feel really on our way. We made Porto Santo in six days arriving in flat calm at 4 a.m, but Porto Santo is well lit and easy to enter so we had no problem entering in the dark. We spent a delightful couple of days there and slipped into that easy relaxed carefree way of life.

But then,we spent the next three nights on anchor watch as the wind piped up to 35 knots from the SW virtually trapping the twenty or so boats in the harbour. There were huge breakers at the mouth and a 6-8ft swell rolling through the anchorage.

Everyone around including ourselves were laying extra anchors down, but due to excellent holding ground only one boat dragged. It was a French boat whose crew had amazingly slept through most of that first night in spite of the fact that the wind was howling and their boat was pitching up and down like a wild donkey. The second amazing thing was the fact that they went through the whole fleet without touching a single boat. It was not until they were 20ft away from the rocks that someone popped their heads out of the hatch wondering what all the fuss was about and why everyone around was shouting and blowing their horns on that dark windy night.

After our seventh day, the weather was back to normal and we pushed onto Madeira. A beautiful island but the marina is something else. We were packed in like sardines eight and nine abreast and the rubbish and filth in the water was a disgrace. The only good thing about it was the fact it killed most of the weed on the bottom of our boat. Who knows they could sell the formula to some anti-fouling paint manufacturer.

Sadie said that we couldn't come to Funchal without a trip on the basket sledges. These are large sledges with steel runners that slide on the cobble stones. A friend, Steve, wanted to come along with us and after a long climb to the top of Funchal town we managed to locate them. The tobogganist was insistent on charging per person which I duly paid. We all climbed into the basket but he could not get the thing moving down the hill. He then indicated for Steve and myself to get out and then proceeded to shoot off with Sadie and the kids. I was non-too happy at being separated, so Steve and I chased after him on foot. We ran behind the sledge for about a mile down the steep hill arriving breathless at the bottom. We tried to explain to him we had paid for a trip on the toboggan and had done nothing more than had a long hot run so could we have our money back please "No problem" he said, "the man at the top of the hill has it!" On being more insistent he then decided he could not speak English so we never did get a refund.

We rented a car and drove up into the mountains. The villages and roads were breathtakingly beautiful clinging to the edge of precarious mountains. We intended to stay a while longer because it's a beautiful island, but got a little fed up with life in the marina. As there was no alternative safe anchorage we sailed off towards Graciosa in the Canaries.

Vicky and James exploring in the Canaries.

We had a splendid sail covering 300 miles in 48hrs without pushing the boat at all. Halfway across I had the fright of my life when our little Vicky pointed out that water was splashing over the edge of the floor boards and her Lego was floating. As the bilges are 18 inches deep it will give you some idea how much water we had taken on board. I spent ten frantic minutes turning off all the stop cocks and trying to trace the source of the leak. After about 20 minutes with two electric bilge pumps going we managed to empty the bilges. To our dismay as soon as I switched off the pumps it started to refill. After the second emptying we resumed the search to spot where the water was coming from. It was then that Sadie spotted bubbles coming up from the actual bilge pump itself. I then realised what was happening.

The boat was heeling and the exit hole was under water causing the water to syphon back in through the pump when it stopped running. Being the stop cock for the bilge pump it was the only one that I hadn't turned off.

On reaching Graciosa we met up with some friends we had met along the way. We spent two days of sheer joy just swimming, sunbathing and partying aboard the magnificent yacht "Asteroid". Mike, the owner, invited the whole anchorage aboard for the evening. The next morning a fisherman asked us if we wanted any fish, but he would not take any money for them, so in the end we compromised and gave him a bottle of wine. He rowed away with a big smile on his face leaving us with more fish than we could eat.

From there through the Canary Islands we cruised in company with the yachts "Tanagra III." "Kirsten Jayne" and "Tamure". Most of our experiences were a delight but unfortunately in Las Palmas "Tamure" was robbed whilst tied alongside us. The thief seeing Kitty (the owner's wife), the children and myself climb off their boat onto ours must have assumed Tamure was empty. Scott, the owner, was working repairing the heads. He heard a noise and to his horror looked around the door to see· a man rummaging through his boat. I heard him shouting from my boat next door and leapt up thinking he had trapped his fingers or something. On reaching my deck I saw the stranger coming out of Scott's boat. I quickly nipped over the rail and grabbed hold of him.

At first Scott assumed he had taken nothing, so was content to simply get him off his boat. He then realised his leather wallet from the chart table containing their passports, ships papers and $200 had gone. We gave chase and managed to catch the thief further along the dock. We held him until the police came and took him away. They took statements from us, but unfortunately the wallet was never recovered. We believe he threw it in the sea when we gave chase.

I think the police had problems making a case stick without evidence, but somehow the thief "accidentally" broke his leg whilst being questioned by the police.Later that night we learned another boat had been robbed, apparently by the same person, so it looked as if he got his just reward for his sins.

Boats seem to be more of a target over the last few years the world over. One has to be as vigilant as possible about your goods and specially to remember to lock dinghies to something solid whilst away from them. It's such a pity in Las Palmas because the authorities are doing their best to accommodate yachts and improve standards all round.

From Las Palmas Gran Canaria we sailed to Tenerife where we had an incredibly cheap haul out and anti-foul at Los Cristianos. The boat sails a full 1.5 knots faster with a clean bottom.

Onward from Tenerife we sailed to La Gomera. The interior of this island must be visited as the scenery is awe-inspiring, with its huge bizarre shaped mountains and rich fertile valleys that grow most tropical fruits you can think of. A ride on the local bus across the island is very reasonable, but don't risk it if you suffer with vertigo as the cliff top roads are quite scary.

The following day we said our goodbyes to our good friends aboard "Tamure" and headed off to La Palma. With a gentle breeze from the West, the sun shining bright, Mozart playing on the stereo, the kids doing their school work with Sadie, it was the nearest thing to heaven I'm ever likely to get. We covered 55 miles to La Palma in 8 hours, motor sailing most of the way.

It was from La Palma we stocked up for the Atlantic crossing with fresh fruit and vegetables from their very reasonable market. We filled the boot of the taxi with sacks of potatoes and oranges , etc. We found an avocado tree laden with unripe fruit, so we picked a few dozen. We also went to the bakery for a sack of flour for bread making. The taxi driver stood scratching his head wondering what on earth we were going to do with it all. When we directed him to the yacht port, a look of enlightenment came over his face

Crossing the Atlantic

Saturday 24th November 1989, the big day, came for us to set off across the Atlantic again. Although it was our third crossing now, the feeling of apprehension and a little fear still enters the pit of our stomachs. On attempting to leave we discovered our stern anchor had snagged on a submerged chain and couldn't be freed without donning the diving bottles. We originally intended to be away for about 12 o'clock but with the last-minute checks, shopping and anchor snag, it was 3 o'clock before we eventually set sail and waved goodbye to our friends and terra firma for a few weeks.

Oily calm sea can drive you mad if it lasts too long.

What a sail we had in the first 24 hours, covering 161 miles, I would have preferred to have started out a little gentler, as our legs and stomachs had become a bit soft due to too much time in harbour. Still, I couldn't help being pleased with our progress.

Our second night at sea was a night best forgotten. With the wind boxing the compass and seas tumbling in a mixed-up motion, we spent the whole night wallowing and rolling with squalls coming through every few minutes or so. In fact, we almost looked forward to the squalls as at least we could get the boat moving in them and the wind in the sails steadied the boat.

The Following day was just as bad with overcast skies, little wind and wallowing seas.We could feel a miserable depression creeping over us, having also to motor for at least 14hours.

I felt very sorry for Sadie as cooking in these conditions was a nightmare, nothing stayed still and pots and pans were scattered around the boat quite regularly. She never ceased to amaze me, how she managed to produce such mouth-watering dishes.

Later on, in the afternoon, the sun came out and a little wind started to fill our flogging sails. Our spirits lifted with the breeze as the rolling diminished to relieve our aching bodies.

A further thing to brighten our day was the landing of the biggest Dorodo fish I have ever seen. It was bigger and stronger than James. Believe this fisherman's story or not, but we hooked one on each line being trailed at the same time. Alas one escaped but the one we landed snapped the rod in half. I was determined not to let the second one beat us. Eventually we managed to get a couple of turns of line around the winch and gently hauled him in using the drum as a clutch whenever the fish dived. Having got the thing alongside the boat, and up to our ankles in line, we were still not sure what to do, so I blindly went after it with the gaff. I braced myself against a shroud and with super human strength pulled it onto the deck. What a shock we had, it leapt around the deck like a shark in a frenzy, with me frantically trying to control it and avoid its huge mouth full of teeth. At the same time I hit it a good one with the winch handle in order to stun it. Finally it was controlled and fully converted into beautiful fresh white steaks ready for the freezer, only to find out the freezer had stopped working. Fortunately, it turned out to be nothing more than a loose wire which was quickly rectified. The thought of losing all the meat gave us a nasty few moments when we were only four days out.

On our fifth day out, we had the opportunity to try out our newly acquired second hand spinnaker, which pulled us along at a steady 4 knots in light airs. The following day we got a little too confident as we left it to fend for itself for most of the morning. With the boat steering on wind pilot steering gear, consequently when the wind almost died altogether we ended up with a spinnaker wrap. After wasting the best part of an hour motoring around in circles to unwrap it. We finally ended up motoring for the rest of the day under bare poles.

The sixth day out will probably remain one of the highlights of my life. Ghosting along at about 2 knots in the sunshine on a flat sea, we were surrounded by dolphins...dozens of them. So, I trailed a rope to make sure the boat did not leave me, then donned my mask and flippers.

What an experience when I first jumped in, about eight or nine of them swam directly underneath me with squeaks coming from different ones, being very audible under water. They seemed quite concerned at me being in the water at first, but within a minute there must have been about twenty all nosing around, but none would come close enough to touch. The sight of those wonderful mammals effortlessly gliding around in the beautiful, crystal water sent a tingle down my spine.

Off to bed after a bedtime story on deck.

There are not enough adjectives to describe the feeling-it was pure pleasure. Through the many thousands of miles we have sailed we never cease to be entertained whenever they pay us a visit.

Sunday 2nd December. Still no wind. Only about 1 or 2 knots from the West. Whoever heard of getting westerlies at 18 degrees North 30 degrees West!!-right in the middle of the easterly trade wind route. Columbus would never have made it in 18 days had he encountered these conditions. The sea is like a mirror with just a rolling swell coming from the North. Unless the trades develop we are going to be hard pressed to make it to Barbados for Christmas. It is a feeling of real isolation and frustration to be hundreds of miles from the nearest land and not a breath of wind to propel you along.

Yesterday the SatNav broke down, so I am now having to rely on my sextant. I worked out my position last night by using Jupiter and the moon without too much problem.

Monday 3rd December. Three o'clock in the morning I am sitting here on my watch with still no sign of trade winds. It is now four days since we managed to sail in the right direction. The motor has been running now for the last 26 hours nonstop. It's enough to drive one mad.

Shark for diner-tasted a bit like Swordfish

Tuesday 4th December. After having the engine run now for 47 hours, a breeze has finally picked up from the East. There must be shouts of hurray from all over the Atlantic. I know that most of the 150 yachts that set off in the ARC race have serious reservations about getting there for Christmas. Only the large boats with long range motoring capacity have made any real progress. We have seen four yachts so far, the smallest being 55 feet. We have spent most of the last few days varnishing all the bright work around the decks, doing all the tricky bits that I never found time for in harbour. Gringo's looking in fine fettle now.

Wednesday 5th December. Today – overcast, dull and miserable. The only good thing about today was the smell of bread baking and the Christmas Cake that Sadie baked. For the last few days I have been experimenting with drying some fish. Surprise, surprise it tasted very good. Since James discovered its savoury taste he seems to be chewing every time I look at him.

Thursday 6th December. Last night was a real wild one with 30 knots of wind on the beam, driving rain and big tumbling seas. I don't think any of us got much sleep. I can remember nodding off on the side of the bunk and waking up with a bump on the cabin floor. The motion was so bad that it was tossing us around like a cork. The day was even worse with the wind moving around until it was bang on the nose. All of us are feeling very depressed at the prospect of being thrown around all day and making no progress west. In my wildest dreams, I would not have thought this would be happening in the middle of the trade wind zone. The skies are still dark and miserable, just the same as our moods.

Friday 7th December. Another overcast day with very little wind and slow progress.

Saturday 8th December. Feeling a little depressed again today, being fed up with the wallowing around and sailing at the pace of a snail. This huge ocean seems to stretch on forever with no method of making headway in the light airs. After days on end of calms, I've come to the conclusion that I would rather be in a gale, provided it came from the right direction.

Sunday 9th December. Hooray, at last the wind has shifted around to the East. It's not very strong but at least it is in the right direction, enabling us to get the spinnaker up for most of the day, also that forgotten treat, sunshine. The first we have seen in three days.

Monday 10th December. Again, we plodded on at about 4 knots throughout the day, spending a pleasant day fishing, sunbathing and generally being lazy. We made contact with the 126ft yacht "Centurion" on the VHF. They all sounded a little despondent as they had made no better time than us so far, and they had charter guests to take on the 24th from Antigua. As they were low on diesel they couldn't motor anymore, so had to be content wallowing around at 2-3knots. To our astonishment we heard the noise of a boat engine and when we looked up a couple of the crew from Centurion waterskied around our boat and with little more than a smile and a wave, returned back to their mother ship. That's the last thing we expected mid Atlantic. Quite an experience I would imagine being over a thousand miles from land.

At the end of the day the little wind we had, ran out as the sun went down and we ended up having to motor all night again.

Tuesday 11th December Hurray, at last we are bounding along again making good progress.

Wednesday 12th December. For over two days and nights we have pressed on towards our destination at sometimes 8 knots. At last the gap is closing as we inch our way across the chart.

Thursday 13th December. Not much sleep last night as we surged up and down on the huge Atlantic swell with the occasional one crashing against the hull jarring everything around our little world.

Me feeling tired, but the kids never ran out of energy

We have logged 2,500 miles but still have over 400 miles to go, thanks to the great dog-leg in our course through trying to find the elusive trade winds, but at last they've arrived and over the last three days we've made good time. That night Vicky came up into the cockpit to inform us that the water pump would not stop running. On investigating I had the bleak realisation that the water tanks were empty. We have about 400 miles still to go and only our reserve water left (15 gallons!). I thought the main tank must have sprung a leak and all our water had drained into the bilges and then been pumped out by the bilge pump!

I worked out that we should survive on our reserve water but thank God it didn't happen a couple of weeks back or we could have been in serious trouble. When I checked into the water matter a little more I discovered an air lock in the feed pipe and the pump wasn't drawing the water from the bottom half of the tank. We hadn't lost any water after all. It gave me a real scare and served to make me keep an eye on the water situation for the future.

Many of the flying fish that flew on board.

Thursday 14th December. Our 20th day at sea. It's been three days since we last did anything to the sails. We've been forging ahead night and day at between 6 and 8 knots relentlessly. According to my calculations we should be sighting Barbados tomorrow night. Already I can feel the excitement welling up inside after so long at sea. It will be nice to stretch our legs and see something other than water around us.

Friday 15th December. Another good day of passage making, even though its very rolly due to the big seas. I was very pleased with myself, landing a yellow fin Tuna. I placed the fish head down in a bucket planning to gut and slice it into steaks when Sadie's turn of watch came around a little later on. To my horror the fish gave an almighty wriggle and managed to tip the bucket over. I could only stand and watch as the fish slipped through the open hatch, dropping down onto Sadie's pillow down below. She was asleep in bed. Never in my life have I ever seen anyone wake up and jump out of bed so quickly. Needless to say she was not amused one bit and had real doubts of the authenticity of my story. Even though all the sheets on the bed were all changed there was still the pong of fish in our cabin. How were we going to explain to the laundrette in Barbados why the pillow case and sheets were covered in blood?! They would never believe our story.

Tonight is the big night and we should spot land if my calculations are correct. The end of a long voyage is always tinged with apprehension as is indeed the start. As we approached Barbados our spirits were lifted at the sound of Christmas Carols on the radio. It inspired Sadie and the children to start making Christmas decorations.

Saturday 16th December 2 a.m the lights of Barbados are on the horizon. On our approach the deck of the yacht was covered in flying fish. I thought it a shame to waste them, so experimented by frying a few up for breakfast. They turned out to be very tasty, but very bony.

Land Ahoy

Hooray for a peaceful night's sleep, with the boat resting too. That's the one thing I'm looking forward to more than anything. Anyway, we checked in 21 days 16 hours after leaving La Palma, knocking one day off our last crossing, which wasn't bad considering the calms mid-Atlantic.

Christmas 1999 in Barbados

On reaching Barbados we learned that two yachts had sunk during their Atlantic crossings. One having the rudder break off and the other hitting a whale. The good news that came from the incidents is that all the people from both yachts were rescued by other yachts and delivered safely to the West Indies.

Within minutes of dropping anchor in Carlisle Bay we all jumped over the side for a swim in the crystal clear warm water of the Caribbean. We spent the next hour scraping away the profusion of goose neck barnacles dangling just below the water line on the transom. We need not have bothered as we found out once the boat stops moving and the flow of water ceases they tend to drop off of their own accord.

We spent Christmas in Barbados. The children were a little concerned how Father Christmas was going to deliver their presents to the boat when we didn't have a chimney. When we told them, the dolphins would take care of that, they seemed quite happy. We intended to spend our New Year in Bequia but the anchorage at Port Elizabeth was so crowded we moved onto Mustique. After two nights in Bequia we were getting fed up of being bumped by charter boats who seemed to drop anchor without consideration as to where the boat might lie. The French were the worst culprits. One, who dropped his hook right in front of us, claimed in French that his engine would not start and that he could not speak English, when asked to move, because his boat was hitting ours. In the end we dropped back to avoid hitting him. The next morning, he started his engine to move off and I asked him in English "how come your engine is running now?" he replied in perfect English "oh I fitted a new ignition switch" so I replied to him "I thought you couldn't speak English last night" to which he just shrugged and left with a sheepish smile on his face.

At Anchor in Mustique

Anyway, we ended up having a super New Year at Basil's Bar in Mustique. We had a barbecue on the beach under a full moon that lit the beach and palm trees like a flood light.

From there on we island-hopped down to Grenada taking in the Tobago Cays with their ice blue water. We found little change since our last visit in any of the islands apart from the increase in charter vessels. In Grenada we met up with a dear friend, Richard Morton, who had arranged a postal address for us at his sister's lovely house, where we were wined and dined in true regal style.

We had a mixture of fun and grief in Grenada. Without consultation, I entered Sadie into the local mixed triathlon that included a run, cycle race and swim. Having always been a strong swimmer that is the part I put her down for. She was non-too pleased when I announced it but she gallantly took part - having to swim out to sea, around an anchored boat and back again - a distance of about a mile. She did not disgrace the Wilkins family and managed second place for her team. She was later presented with a medal by the Tourist Minister for Grenada.

The next day was not so good for us as James managed to cut his chin at the local swimming pool. He was taken to the local hospital to have some stitches put in, being watched by Sadie (an ex-theatre nurse). She had seen many an operation in her time but watching her own son being stitched was too much for her and she collapsed in a heap on the floor, taking all the attention away from poor James. Needless to say she did not live that down for quite a time.

After Grenada we sailed onto the island of Margarita which is part of Venezuela. Venezuela is a must for any yachtsman coming this way. In fact we were astonished at the low cost of living here because we received such a good exchange rate for our money. The Venezuelan currency is Bolivars of which there are approximately 100 to the pound. A labourer only earns about 100 Bolivars per day.

A trip to the jungle

In Cumana Marina (mainland Venezuela) we got friendly with a guard who was keen to improve his English, so we invited him on board for drinks. We sorted out a few of the children's old books as they were very basic and ideal for his learning. Everywhere in these types of countries guards are well armed and he was no exception- arriving on board with his machine gun, which he placed on the table, much to my James' delight. I couldn't believe it when he gave it to him to play with saying "it's no problem the safety catch is on" pointing to where the safety catch was. I had visions of holes being blown in the side of the boat or even worse. Needless to say I had to take it off James, much to his disappointment. The guard thought it was funny. How can powers that be give arms to such irresponsible people? However, he did take care of our boat while we went off to the Amazon. We caught a bus to Ciudad Bolivar, a distance of about 500 kms and it only cost us $3.80 for the 8-hour trip. In Ciudad Bolivar we stayed in a hotel overlooking the Orinoco River at a cost of $16 for the four of us for the night. That night we met up with a man who said he was a diamond dealer and dressed very much like Indiana Jones. I had my doubts about what he really did so in the evening, after a few drinks, I asked him how he paid for his diamonds. To my amazement he said, "Oh I have money sewn into my clothes" and proceeded to pick open a pocket to expose a wad of hundred dollar notes. He went on to tell us how the traders sent armed guards to escort him to and from the mines, as it is in their interest to protect him. He then went on to show us some diamonds he had already bought. My thoughts were that at any minute he was going to offer to sell some to me but he never did. I was sure the next morning when he was more sober he must have thought what the hell was I doing last night, what a risk.

From there we caught a plane to the Cumana Indian reservation which was only discovered in the late 1940s and still has no roads leading to it. The cost of the plane was £23 return, but you have to remember that fuel was only £0.05p a gallon.

La Gran Sabana, in which it is located consists of 7.4 million acres. We stayed three nights with an Indian family who acted as our guides and cooked our meals for us.

When we paid them $20 for three night's stay, it was more money than they had ever seen. During this time, we went on a 20-mile canoe trip up the river Carro, that wound its way through dense jungle and huge flat-topped mountains with the occasional waterfall thundering down into the river. At night we slept in hammocks that took a little getting used to. At least it kept us clear of the many huge creepy crawlies, the worst of which were giant ants about an inch long which gave a really vicious bite.

The Cumanamai Family who looked after us.

The day time was very hot, but the nights were really cold, so we had to sleep with all our clothes on and wrapped in a couple of blankets. There is no room for luxuries as everything has to be carried on your back, so you only take the essentials. When we left our jungle airport we took a detour to visit the Angel Falls, the highest waterfalls in the world at 3,212 feet high - 15 times higher than Niagara Falls. From the Angel Falls the pilot allowed me to fly our little Cessna back to Ciudad Bolivar. I tried to explain to him I had only had a couple of flying lessons. His English was limited and my Spanish was non-existent. Whether he got the wrong impression and thought I could fly, I'm not sure, but he let me take over the controls. He pointed out the compass heading, altitude and artificial horizon etc.

After about an hour the pilot was having a little nap and left things to me which was fine until I looked ahead and saw cloud. The first cloud I just skirted around but the second cloud was much bigger so I decided to fly straight through keeping a careful eye on the altitude and artificial horizon etc. At this point a young German traveller, who had hitched a lift with us, asked Sadie about my flying skills. When she told him I had only ever had one lesson "oh my God" came from him in perfect English. Fortunately, the clouds then cleared, so on I flew toward Ciudad Bolivar, with the pilot now sound asleep and our hitch-hiker friend still in a terrible sweat. After a while I thought I better wake the pilot and gave him a little shake to wake him up. He didn't seem to be bothered and proceeded to put a couple of eye drops into each eye. When I eventually got him to take over and orientate himself to my amazement he then started to descend. We were little more than 10 minutes from our destination.

Our Jungle beds were quite comfortable once you mastered getting in them.

From there we headed east to visit the joining of the two great rivers of Orinoco and the Caroni at Puerto Ordaz. Here millions of gallons of water combine in a tremendous concoction of whirlpools and turbulence on their journey to the Orinoco Delta, where it discolours the ocean for hundreds of square miles with its amber coloured water. We then had another plane journey to Barcelona, on the North coast of Venezuela, and then took a battered old 1950s American car with just about everything on the car rattling. The cost was the equivalent of £4 to get back to our yacht. I felt that was far too little to pay so I gave him an extra £5. I did not expect him to put his arms around me and give me a hug.

Off along the Colombian Coast

From Cumana we pushed west again, sailing to the island of Tortuga, an island about the size of Guernsey but completely uninhabited, apart from the few fishermen camping on the beach. Uninhabited islands always have a strange eerie feel to them somehow. Over the next eleven days we were to become acquainted with several such places. Over that period of time we never saw a sign of life ashore at seven different anchorages. Because human life in these areas is so sparse the life in the sea thrives with an incredible profusion of fish and coral.

The group of islands Los Roques is probably the finest unspoilt cruising ground left in the world. There are ice blue waters and exquisite lagoons that hold new delights galore for yachtsmen and divers alike. The one anchorage there with the name of "Lanqui Canareo" is described in the pilot book as the best anchorage in the world and I can well believe that.

On leaving the beautiful Los Roques, after 5 lazy days of diving and beach parties, we set sail for the ABC Islands via Les Aves. Again a lovely group of tiny islands off the Venezuela coast, supposed to be rich in lobsters but unfortunately we never found any. It looked a bit tricky to go to the outer reef with a heavy swell crashing down on it. Hence, we gave the lobsters a miss this time.

After an early start, we reached the first in the line of the ABC group of Dutch Antilles being Bonaire. An island run in true Dutch style with its clean pleasant town and good waterside restaurants. Over the last few years Bonaire has developed a booming tourist trade in scuba diving. The waters around the reefs are crystal clear and the reefs themselves are as beautiful as any I've seen. The whole area has been designated as a National Park and no fishing is allowed, so there is an abundance of tame tropical fish for divers to admire.

A dive we did in Bonaire on a shipwreck was amazing. About 70 feet down we gained access into the bridge, hold and engine room - it was very eerie but incredibly exciting with fish of every description including a huge moray eel.

Curacao is a much more populated island than Bonaire but has no real place for yachts to stay near the town. Therefore most of the yachts stay in Spanish waters, about 10 miles SE, with an irregular bus service to town. The best method of transport was to hire a car from the very friendly Serafundi marina at reasonable rates. Willemstad proved to be an interesting town though with it's floating market and two bridges that are worlds apart. One being the old Queen Emma pontoon bridge built in 1888 which opens three times a day to let ships and boats through by swinging in a great arc with a tug boat attached to it. The other being the Queen Juliana Bridge recently constructed at a cost of $30 million and 185 ft. above water. It took 14 years and 15 lives to complete with an overall weight of 3,400 tons.

Boisterous seas, but fantastic speed along the Columbian Coast.

After 4 days in Spanish Harbour we felt the urge to get going again. The weather had not been too kind over the last few days with strong winds but, after enquiring for a forecast, I was told this is quite normal for this time of year. So off we set with 25 knots of wind speeding us on our way. In the first 24 hours, we did our best run ever covering 172 miles. Over the next three days we hit the strongest wind yet endured on Gringo, with speeds of 40 knots and gusts up to 54 knots all night with the accompanying sea to match. On the second night disaster struck when our forestay parted at the mast head in spite of the fact that most of the sail was rolled in. Only the halyard connected to the top of the sail stopped the roller gear from falling overboard. For the next three days, we held our breath surfing down 20ft rollers at 6-7 knots with only a storm sail flying on the inner stay.

The local dress of the Cuna Indians with beautiful intricate needlework.

At this present speed we would reach the San Blas Islands at night. Being completely surrounded by reefs it made the prospect a near impossibility especially in these seas. So I set about slowing the boat down by trailing long warps behind. After experimenting with longer and longer warps in a great loop I finally got the boat down to an average of 4 knots. At this speed we should reach the San Blas Islands about 9 a.m, which proved so over the next 48 hours. This was one trip we were glad to get through. All the pilot books warn it can be the roughest part of a circumnavigation. I have no doubt that the big tumbling seas could have easily overwhelmed a small yacht. It was one time I was really glad to have a strong heavy yacht with its long keel for directional stability. Not once over the four days did she ever get out of control and always felt safe.

The Cuna Indians that inhabit the San Blas Islands are a real pleasure to meet being of a natural, friendly disposition. With very few visitors, a couple of local men offered to take us fishing for lobster in their dugout canoe. The canoe was made from a single piece of wood about 30 ft. long with a 6 h.p outboard on the stern. I was amazed how easily driven they are - with four people aboard we could still hold a speed of about 10 knots with ease. On arriving at the desired reef we donned mask and flippers and away we went. Within half an hour we had all the lobster and crab we could eat for the next three days. Would you let a stranger on your island and then go and show him where to catch your lobsters and crabs? The people of the San Blas Islands are truly kind with no prejudices towards anyone. They live in huts made from bamboo and coconut palms with very few worldly possessions [the lucky ones have their own canoe], but they were very happy people always ready with a smile, simply because they don't go hungry due to the profusion of fish.

The local children were incredibly inquisitive. One interesting thing that happened is when Sadie showed them an old instamatic camera, the type where you took the photograph, pull the card out of the back and the picture gradually appears. We took a photo of a group of children and gave them the photo as it started to self-develop. Their eyes became like saucers as they watched the picture appear. I don't believe they had ever seen a photo of themselves before. It was a lovely thing to witness.

What a contrast it was 70 miles along the coast to Colon, the entrance to the Panama Canal with overnight stops at Grand Isle and Portello. En route from Colombia to Panama the ocean has 3,000 miles to build up in the trade wind belt. We sailed for three days until we reached Panama with our nerves on edge with this rig. It was a massive relief to arrive into port.

We had to get the rigging sorted so I made a link call on the SSB (single side band) radio, via Miami, to Rotastay in the UK and managed to order a mast head fitting called an Acmo Toggle. Within a week the part arrived through Fedex. We had a knock on the hull while anchored off the Panama yacht club - "Package for Gringo" we heard. The postman had borrowed a dingy to row out to us, what an amazing service. After an hour or so up the mast all was made good and it gave us no more trouble throughout the rest of the trip.

The notorious Colon is an eye opener. It appears the buildings in the area have never seen any maintenance since the day they were built. Quite a few have bullet holes all over the fascias, the relics of gun battles during the days of Manuel Noriega. The shops are all guarded by security men with machine guns, even the bakery had a man on the door with a pump action shot gun. If you go to a shop in Colon you take a taxi, have the taxi wait outside whilst the armed guard ushers you in and out of the shop, and you never travel in a taxi without locking the doors. The streets are lined with rubbish that stinks something awful in the heat with hoards of young children playing amongst it. It is truly incredible the conditions a human can survive in. It must be a constant battle for survival with law and order virtually gone and the constant risk of disease. With the population exploding God only knows what is to become of such places in a few years time

The Panama Canal to the Galapagos

The Panama Canal itself is a remarkable feat of engineering. The canal rises to a height of 85 ft. above sea level, with locks 1000 feet long and 110 feet across. A total of 26 million gallons of water with each opening and closing of a gate to fill or empty only takes 10 minutes through the massive culverts underground. The doors each weigh 730 tons.

Gringo rafted in the Panama Canal lock with "Kirsten Jayne" and "Finback"

In the years between 1907 and 1914 when the canal was built the problems faced by the Americans must have seemed insurmountable. It was the biggest excavation ever undertaken to that date including the biggest lake at Gatun. In the first few years 22,000 people lost their lives through malaria and yellow fever. A further 5,609 people lost their lives due to accidents. To this day it stands as a great monument of man's determination and ingenuity to achieve the almost impossible. The trip through was most enjoyable with our pilot and four line handlers borrowed from the US Navy. They turned out to be very friendly and helpful people who did it just for the fun of the trip. One lad who came with us had been in the navy for 8 years and this was the first time he had ever been afloat on a boat of any type - he was only involved with land based activities.

Our two days through with a night stop at Gatun Lake eventually brought us out to the Pacific. Under the Bridge of the Americas that links the North and South continents of America, the Pacific stood before us with its awesome distances ahead

We set off after some final provisioning at Balboa, as it would be the last chance for 4,000 miles. We spent the first night at anchor off the little island of Tabaga to settle down before the start of our mammoth leg via the Galapagos Islands. This is often called the "milk run" as gales are very rare and currents are generally in your favour.

Trying to entertain Vicky and James when crossing the Equator

So on the 24th March we upped anchor for the Galápagos Islands. On the 30th we crossed the Equator for the first time at 8.45 a.m and had our little ceremony of dressing up as King Neptune and dousing

Vicky and James with water [Sadie hid behind the camera]. Our spirits were high now as we hoped to sight the islands tomorrow after days of glorious sailing in flat seas and gentle trade winds, occasionally a bit too gentle to make a reasonable speed, but a very agreeable gentle motion. At day break on the 31st March we were five miles off San Cristobal Island, the first for us in the Galapagos Group, after seven days at sea and 707 miles logged.

Landfall in the Galapagos

The Galapagos Isles

On this glorious Sunday morning we cut close to the land to be greeted by some of the seal population along with a few large bottle nosed dolphins. As the sun gradually filled the sky the light turned from deep red to silver.

On the journey along the coast we sailed close to the little island of Leon Durmiente to see the breeding colony of Frigate Birds and Blue Footed Boobies. The sight of those 484ft. cliffs [chart information] only a few yards away, with the birds soaring around the sheer ledges, was really fantastic.

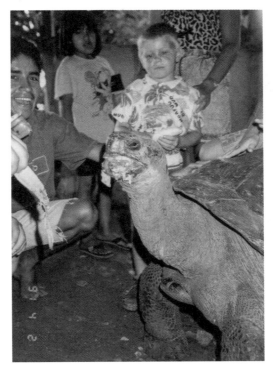

Pepe loved eating bananas

Having dropped anchor in San Cristobal the customs officer came and collected our papers and after that we never saw anyone until Tuesday. Being Easter Sunday the Porto Captain was off for a couple of days. The Ecuadorians at first appear very strict on the time you are allowed to stay and on Tuesday we were more than pleased to be allocated another days stay. A few people around European waters complain of seagulls landing on their boats but here you have to put up with sea lions jumping in your dinghy if you leave it tied behind the boat. We found this out the second night there. We couldn't understand where all the water was coming from. It was not until one night our friends on "Kirsten Jayne" saw one jump into our dinghy to have a snooze for the night. In spite of their weight no damage was done.

During our four days we crammed as much in as possible. We visited one of the giant tortoises, who obligingly gave Vicky and James a ride on his huge back. He weighed over 500lbs so the kids must have felt like mere flies on his back. The gentle giant "Pepe" was said to be 106 years old. We also discovered that bananas were his favourite food. We had to be careful if we wanted to retain our fingers whilst feeding him though.

Another day we had a trip on one of the local boats to the island of Santa Fe with its unique Iguanas and friendly sea lions, being so tame they allow you to stroke them. One rolled on his back to have his belly scratched just like a dog. You do have to keep an eye out for the bull who parades up and down periodically to round up his harem and chases away any stray bulls who venture near. We swam with dozens of sea-lions for about an hour who seemed to have great fun enjoying the experience as much as us. They never showed any sign of aggression coming up and sniffing our hand, corkscrewing in the water around us close enough to touch. It was truly a remarkable experience. Throughout history man has slaughtered these animals for their blubber and skin and yet they are still so friendly toward us. On the beach at Santa Fe we had a fantastic time with the seals who were incredibly inquisitive while we were swimming. Showing no inhibitions whatsoever, they would swim right up to you as if inviting you to play. At one stage on the shore we were surrounded by seals and prehistoric looking marine iguanas. Coming back from Santa Fe, on the trip boat we had been on, the weather very quickly turned foul with 25-30 knots springing up on the nose. It turned out to be the most dangerous part of the whole circumnavigation. Santa Fe is about 30 miles from San Cristobal and the trip boat was totally inadequate for such a voyage. It was ok while the seas were calm but when we were pushing into steep seas it was a different story.

Things started to break, including the crew. They were all being sea sick and then the steering broke. They were so lucky that the passengers were all yachties who had their sea legs. I spent fifteen minutes with my head down the transom and managed to fix the steering rod back on to the rudder stock. We then spent the next two hours beating into a heavy sea in a boat held together with rusty nails. Thank God the engine kept going. They should have paid us for saving their boat, never mind us paying them. Still it was another of life's experiences. I am sure he will never cast off again without being properly prepared.

Treated with total indifference by the local seal colony, but had to keep an eye open for the bull!!

The Ecuadorians are undoubtedly cashing in on these unique islands, as dollars can buy as much time as you would like there. The supposed 72 hours stay on yachts can be extended if you are prepared to pay through the nose to use one of the local tour boats. So long as they keep the islands as they are it's well worth it, but the lucrative tourist trade is already causing the population to increase with restaurants and hotels springing up in the settlements. Let's just hope they limit it in the not to distant future.

We eventually stocked up with diesel, water, vegetables and fruit ready for the longest leg of our journey so far over 3,000 miles to the Marquesas.

The Milk Run

Thursday 4th April. At 4.30 in the afternoon we upped anchor for our mammoth trip across the Pacific with more than a few butterflies in our stomachs. We edged out of Wreck Bay, San Cristobal bound for the open ocean.

Note the little bit of headsail poled out to direct wind into the spinnaker ad help keep it steady in light airs.

Friday 5th April. The next day we had a serious set-back. On my daily inspection of the boat I noticed that the goose neck fitting that attaches the boom to the mast had almost broken away. It was being held on by only ½ inch of weld with about 5 inches of weld broken. Fortunately, me being a bit of a magpie keeping bits and pieces that one day may come in useful, I had some strips of stainless steel plate. I managed to bend it into shape and bolt it all together and affect quite a good mend. It wasn't quite as easy as I have made it sound as it took me the best part of the day to finish. No sooner had that job been done then the roller headsail jammed at the mast head,wrapping the halyard around the forestay. By this time it was getting dark and much too dangerous to get up and fix it. We had to travel through the night with full headsail and hope the wind didn't come up too strong.

Repairing the goose neck. It lasted all the way across the Pacific.

Saturday 6th April. We still had a lumpy sea but the trip up the mast could wait no longer. I went up with Sadie on the winch and Vicky tailing the halyard. We left the main sail set so as to reduce the rocking. When I got up there, 55 feet above the sea, the motion was so violent I had great difficulty just hanging on drawing on all my reserves of strength. I managed to free the offending halyard and tie it back to the mast. It wasn't until I returned to deck that I realised I was covered in scratches and bruises after my epic climb.

Sunday 7th April. The wind piped up a little to steady our restless sails and give us a better ride. Again, we had got so used to the flat seas and smooth canal transit that our bodies developed the familiar ache and tiredness of long distance yachtsmen, but it normally wears off after a few days. Now the seas had become lumpy again and the next few days passed by pretty much one the same as the next, with the occasional squid or flying fish landing on deck.

According to reference books, flying fish do not fly, but glide. Anyone who has spent time at sea in a small boat I'm sure will tell you different. When they emerge from the water they definitely increase speed and often fly about 500 feet.

Wednesday 10th April. In the morning we saw the biggest school of Tuna to date. There were hundreds of them crossing our path about 50 feet in front of the boat.

Today we also received the rather worrying news that two yachts in the Europa '92 race had gone missing and no radio contact had been made with either of them for the last 24 hours. The last message received was that one yacht was being circled by a Korean fishing ship. The second yacht went to investigate and neither have been heard of since. We just hope that it is only radio trouble but the circumstances do sound very suspicious, and we have to pass through that area.

Thursday 11th April. We have been at sea now for seven days and not yet seen sign of life apart from the odd bird or massive shoal of tuna. Not one ship or yacht. It's a real feeling of isolation but Gringo is still pushing on west for us, averaging about 140 miles a day. We still have two-thirds to go (about 2050 miles).

Friday 12th April. Today we had good news and tragic news. The two yachts unaccounted for in the Europa race have both been contacted and are okay. The tragic news is that one of the crew from another yacht has been lost over board hit by the boom. In spite of a 24 hours search by several boats, he was never found. The thought of having to sail on with the loss of a person must be dreadful. If only a preventor had been fitted. The force at which a boom can swing across a deck in 15 knots of wind is phenomenal.

Saturday 13th April. Nine days at sea and making good progress, the weather and the wind being constant now for the last week with good sailing day after day.

Every morning I would have an inspection around the deck to check shrouds, halyards, sails etc for wear and chafe. On stepping onto the foredeck it was covered in bluish stains. On further inspection splodges could be seen all over the foresail to a height of about 15ft. The only thing I could think it might be was squid ink. I looked over the bows of the hull to see that ink was all over the front. The bobstay, an inch diameter solid bar had a slight bend in it. We never felt any bump or jolt in the night but we had without doubt hit something. Was it a giant squid or not? I'll never know, but I couldn't put it down to anything else.

Sunday 14th April. Bowling along in clear blue seas. When the going is like this crossing oceans is no hardship at all. In the evening we had a large shoal of dolphins with us who stayed most of the night, speeding along playing their usual games and leaving great streams of phosphorescent lighting behind them.

A rather unwelcome storm ahead.

Monday 15th April. The skies have been overcast for most of the day, but the wind remains constant. The only thing to note was the sighting of a huge oil tanker on his way to Honolulu who had a friendly chat with us on the VHF.

Mid-Pacific I had a problem with a filling coming out of my tooth. We were well prepared and had emergency tooth filler, but when I read the instructions it said the tooth had to be perfectly dry for it to work properly. Now this is easier said than done and I scratched my head trying to think of a way to dry it out. Eventually I came up with the idea of a bicycle pump, which we had on board. It must have looked a comical sight with me lying on my back, mouth wide open and Sadie pumping away with the pump in my mouth directed at the problem tooth and me trying to hold a mirror at the same time. However I managed to do the job, much to my relief, and believe it or not it was still sound when we reached New Zealand and I had the tooth filled properly.

Tuesday 16th April. Still sailing along making good time. We've hardly changed the sails now for six days apart from putting a reef in the main at night. At sea one has lots of time to think and dream.

One of the great things about long distance sailing is that the time spent at sea you really are yourself. No one to impress, no one to prove anything to, everything is for real. You gradually come to expect less and less and small trifling things become a source of satisfaction. For instance, the catching of a fish or the smell of a freshly baked loaf of bread can brighten up your whole day. Perhaps that is the secret of true living. A flashy new car or a million pounds in the bank doesn't mean a thing out here, but a loaf of bread or a cup of water sustains your life. The gains of sailing round the world go far beyond seeing beautiful places.

Wednesday 17th April. Had a bit of an uncomfortable night with the wind falling light and a rolling sea which results in the sails banging to and fro. Nothing grates on my nerves more than that infernal bang from the sails.

In the morning we changed the sail configuration to run a poled out headsail and cruising chute. The boat steadied herself and sailed a lot better when the wind backed to the East. By mid-afternoon we were back to our old-rig again. The wind was just playing tricks on us.

Thursday 18th April. Things have improved a little with slightly better wind and steady sailing.

Friday 19th April. The boat is now finding it hard going due to the amount of dreaded gooseneck barnacles. She is making nowhere near her hull speed - we must be at least 2 knots down on average. When it is quiet at night you can hear the water slushing along the hull rather than flowing. We are going to have a real cleaning off job when we reach Hiva Oa.

Saturday 20th and Sunday 21st April. Funny but I still get the feeling of 'the weekend's here'. On Saturday morning I think of my brothers and Dad going for a Saturday lunchtime pint. Perhaps it's a touch of home sickness. Sunday was the slowest day's progress yet with about 7-8 knots of wind all day and lazy blue skies. We had the most beautiful sunset, the whole of the western sky going a deep reddish purple after the big red sun dipped down below the horizon.

Monday 22nd April. Still plodding along slowly with overcast sky. The gap is gradually closing on the chart. We've tried for the last three days to contact the outside world on the SSB radio but to no avail. We hope our parents aren't too worried. We've been at sea now for almost three weeks and still have over 500 miles to go.

Tuesday 23rd April. Last night was very frustrating with very light airs, not enough to fill the sails and constantly changing direction. So, in the end, we gave up the struggle and motored all night. At least it boosted our hard-worked batteries.

Another glorious Pacific night

Wednesday 24th April. Pulling along at a steady 3 knots. We would have been making another 2 knots at least but our hull is so badly fouled with barnacles. It's a bit like driving a car with the hand brake on. If the slow pace seemed frustrating it was nothing compared to the day time with squall after squall passing through. The wind was constantly changing direction and strength. We must have changed the sails 20 times during the hours of daylight. At one time the whole sky went black and we really expected something very nasty but the worst we got was 30 knots of wind for about 5 minutes. One minute overcast, next minute bright sunshine, we didn't even know how to dress for the day. It may not sound hard work, but with the lack of sleep as well it gradually wears you down. We ended up motoring all night again.

Thursday 25th April. Our third week out from the Galapagos Islands. Last night we decided to sleep on deck. We made our bed up, very comfortable too, looking up to the stars until a squall came over and the heavens opened. The Lord above must have had a good laugh at us just nodding off and then being rudely awakened with lashings of rain, grabbing pillows and blankets etc. and running for cover. It was difficult getting to sleep again after that. The morning again was very frustrating sailing wise with constantly varying light winds. However, we managed to sail in the afternoon with just the spinnaker flying. By evening the wind died away forcing us to either wallow around or start the old engine. It was most uncomfortable with the big rolling sea and no wind. We were cheered up though, because we managed to phone home; believe it or not, we made a link call through Portishead. To make a call to England via Portishead is nigh on a miracle as a series of skip distances have to be exact. That is the radio waves do a series of bounces from the sea to the sky and then end up at the desired server if you are very lucky. During Sadie's watch she came to me to say she could hear Portishead radio, "impossible" I said, but just as I went to the radio I heard a voice say "Portishead clear. Anymore calls." I replied giving my position and the radio operator replied back saying "I think you are a little confused, as you have put yourself in the middle of the Pacific". "I am in the middle of the Pacific" I replied. "Oh", he said "that is amazing, give us a count to ten and I will get you even clearer". I then gave Sadie's Mum's number – she was out. I then gave my Mum and Dad's number and my Dad answered, he is in his late 80's and all he could tell me was that "your Mum is at the hairdresser". He had no conception of how lucky I had been to make that call but at least it was nice to hear his voice. Five minutes later we lost contact. We never did manage another call. However, it really did lift our spirits.

Friday 26th April. Again we had to motor last night, but at last we had a breeze spring up from the East early in the morning. I did a very stupid trick trying to hoist the spinnaker too quickly. With one eye cocked on the spinnaker I hauled away almost to the top intending to quickly put some turns on the winch, when I was at the desired height, as I had done so many times before, but the spinnaker filled before I had chance to cleat off the halyard, it lifted me about 4 feet from the deck (the spinnaker is 1,800 sq ft.) I had no choice but to let go. The spinnaker inevitably went under the boat breaking the spinnaker pole and getting into an almighty mess with sheets and fishing lines. The whole mess tangled up under the boat, but fortunately it didn't foul on the prop. After half an hour of struggling Sadie, Vicky and myself managed to retrieve everything with only the loss of a few meters of fishing line and a few small tears in the spinnaker. Within an hour we were on our way again under the cruising chute and stay sail. A little slower than we would have been with the spinnaker set. We now have less than 200 miles to go so it's not too drastic. We saw our first flock of birds today, the first for three weeks. A sure sign of closing in on land.

Diner for the next couple of days. A large Wahoo.

Saturday 27th April. Had a reasonable day's sail with clear blue skies and gentle breeze. If we can keep the boat moving at 4 knots we should be in Hiva Oa by lunchtime tomorrow. The fact that the boat has sailed so slowly over the past few days, has caused this last leg to drag a little. We are all looking forward to seeing land now. We have been at sea for 31 days and nights with only 4 nights break in the Galapagos. We are beginning to feel a bit weary now.

Land Ahoy - The Marquesas

Sunday 28th April. 6 o'clock in the morning LAND AHOY!!!!
As the sun came up after one of the best nights at sea I've ever experienced. A true South Pacific evening with a full moon and cloudless sky. We had about 12 knots of wind steady all night. What better landfall could we have had after our marathon voyage. By 2 p.m. we were safely anchored in Taahuka Bay, Hiva Oa, French Polynesia to give its full title. Oh, for a full night's sleep-what bliss. A few friends were already here to greet us and the bay looks beautiful.

Anchored in Hiva Oa. Looking forward to a good nights sleep.

On venturing up the hill towards the tiny village, after ten paces along the road a pickup stopped to give us a lift. This was to be the friendly way the people were throughout French Polynesia. The only thing that we didn't like about the place was the heavy bond you have to put up, which is refundable on leaving the island. For us it cost $8,400-for some families this must represent a real problem.
After savouring the delightful atmosphere of the place for a few days, we moved on to Tahuata, where the locals laid on a banquet for the

handful of yachts in the bay. It consisted of goat meat, lobster, fish, bananas in coconut sauce and we were to discover at all these feasts there is always four times more food than the guests can eat.

At Hana Manu on the North coast of Hiva Oa, an anchorage we were not really bothered about going to, was a convenient stop off on our way to Ua Huka. It turned out to be a sailor's dream, with a beautiful waterfall and fresh fruit of all types growing wild for the taking. We ended up staying three days. The only drawback with this place were the vicious insects known as nosee'ems. They bite like mosquitos but are too small to see. Compared to the beautiful surroundings though it was a small price to pay.

Two Local lads help me make a makeshift Spinnaker Pole. They were always willing to lend a hand.

Another unwelcome visitor to the bay were sharks. A friend on a boat "Wild Wind" moored near us, caught a small shark as dusk descended, so I decided to try my luck, without much success. After an hour I gave up, but left the line and hook with a piece of meat dangling over the side. At 3 a.m. we were rudely woken by a banging noise on the side of the hull. On investigation, we saw a 6 ft. white tip shark had taken the bait and was thrashing widely around in the water alongside the boat. I was bewildered what to do or how to handle it but the problem solved itself after ten minutes when the shark managed to bite through the steel trace with his mouth full of sharp teeth. Anyway, we stocked Gringo with bananas, limes, oranges, breadfruit, paw-paw, coconuts and mangos.

This anchorage was once a heavily populated area, but is now deserted after a hurricane in 1945. It's amazing how quickly the jungle reclaims a place. The only traces left are numerous foundations of houses and the rows of coconut trees with lead bands around the trunks to stop rats from climbing them. Everything else is completely overgrown.

A natural paradise with clear water and fresh fruit growing all around.

We left Hana Manu at 3 a.m feeling our way out of the bay in the dark to the open ocean bound for Ua Huka. On arriving there we were greeted by a formidable looking entrance and a rolly harbour. Nevertheless, we dropped anchor and went ashore to the pleasant little village. We wandered around and met a few friendly inhabitants.

On arriving back at the boat the swell had built up to 4 feet, making the anchorage too dangerous for my liking, so off we set just as darkness was descending, bound for Nuka Hiva. At 12 midnight we were safely anchored at Controller Bay after very slowly edging our way in using radar and Sadie's excellent night vision, standing on the bow giving directions. We awoke the next morning to a glorious sunny day with fantastic surroundings and feeling much happier after a good night's sleep. We later moved on to the main harbour and spent a very pleasant week there, spending our time dining out at the Keikahanui Inn in the evening and horse riding during the day. One unusual pig at the riding stables was convinced he was a dog. Every time we went there he came running up to us along with two dogs wagging his curly tail. If anyone stroked him he would roll over on his back for you to tickle his belly in competition with the two dogs. In fact, whenever visitors arrived the pig always managed to take the limelight from the rest of the animals there, to his great satisfaction.

One problem we encountered during our visit was the fact we were following the Europa Round the World yacht race. They seemed to swamp the little village and buy everything in sight, including all the diesel, petrol and gas. When the supply ship arrived a week later all was returned to normal.

Daniel is always a friend to yachtsmen - a true gentleman.

Our main highlight of Nuka Hiva was a trip to the water fall from Daniel's Bay. We were escorted by Daniel himself along one of the most beautiful walks you could ever imagine. We hiked through the tropical forest and then though a great gorge with vertical walls about 1,000 ft high.

Even though Daniel must be around 70 years of age he still took a lot of keeping up with. He set the pace over the rough terrain, including the crossing of a few knee-deep rivers. The five-mile walk started at 7 a.m to avoid the hot sun. It certainly gave us an appetite when we returned. Later on that day we took Daniel a few groceries to show our gratitude only to be presented in return with a quarter of a goat. I wonder how much longer these people can sustain this generosity with the ever-increasing number of yachts coming to the area.

James is not too happy sitting on the Sacrificial Alter

Our next island was Ua Pou after a brisk day sailing across. We entered the little harbour and were greeted by several cruising yachties who had become friendly with us along the way. The following day [Sunday] a visit to the local church was in order to listen to the choir. Their natural harmony can make the hairs stand up on the back of your neck. It really is lovely. The next day one of the locals took us in his Land Rover up into the mountains. We visited the remains of ancient villages and an old altar in the jungle where human sacrifices were once offered up. It really was like something from a film set and very eerie.

According to historians it has been 100 years since human sacrifice was practiced here. In fact, the Marquesans Islands were one of the last places on earth where cannibals lived apparently.

Sailing the dangerous Isles

On the 21st May we set sail for the Tuamotus Islands or Dangerous Islands as Captain Cook called them, due to the fact that they were mainly low-lying atolls and reefs that are difficult to spot until close up. Also, there is a problem of strong currents around the area. Our first day's sail was just a dream with a steady 12 knots on the beam. In fact, we never took the cruising chute down for 36 hours. The boat was so steady in the flat sea, we had difficulty detecting we were moving at all. It was like sitting in a marina. Our second night was a little different with squall after squall passing through every hour or so with torrential rain. The rain came down so hard it was difficult to breathe in it while reducing sail. It was cold, being in the state of unprepared attire, as most night watches we just wear shorts and T shirt.

On reaching Takaroa we met up with our old friends Basil and Angela on the yacht "Cutaway" whom we first met in Antigua in 1988. Sadie noticed they had a small coconut tree growing in a bucket. You could see it sprouting nicely from the original coconut. She had admired it a couple of times and when we were ashore there were hundreds of them everywhere, so she chose a nice one just like Basil's and brought it back to the boat. The next night we invited Basil and Angela over for a sundowner and Sadie proudly showed them her new little tree. "Where did you get it from?" asked Basil. "Oh just alongside the path going into the village. It came up very easily", she said. On closer inspection Basil started to laugh. "It's the one I planted in memory of a friend who I once visited this island with. He had a wicked sense of humour and would have seen the funny side of that!! Of all the coconut trees in Takaroa, you picked one I had planted. I had wondered where it had gone".

The pearl industry seems to have taken over the whole village, everyone except the shop keeper seems to be involved with it. The whole lagoon has been divided up between the local families for the production of cultured pearls, most of which are exported to Japan. After a little arm bending Sadie talked me into buying her one of the beautiful black pearls that the island is so famous for. In spite of the numerous dives we did we failed to find one in its natural state, even though we found a few oysters. It was quite a hairy experience at times diving in these waters as they abound with sharks and several dives had to be aborted due to white and black tip sharks pestering us.

In the centre of the Tuamotus Island lies Kauehi atoll. It turned out to be pure bliss - just as you would imagine a south sea island with crystal blue waters and palm fringed beaches. We found real virgin Islands and over a three-night stay we never saw another human anywhere.

We toured other islands in the group including Fakarava and Toau, each with its own bit of magic. Toau for instance only has seven residents. They made us very welcome to their insular world, a visitor made a real change for them. Alas, even paradise can have a sting in its tail and, on our third night there, a blow came up from the South and made our anchorage uncomfortable and risky.

Demonstrating how the grain of sand is implanted in the Oyster to create a Pearl.

One of the nights we met up with the Yachts "Wild Wind" and "Kirsten Jayne". In the evening, we were invited over to "Wild Wind" and after dinner decided to have a fishing competition. Within minutes I pulled out a small shark. A few minutes later, after a long struggle, Denis off "Wild Wind" pulled another one out. A good-sized shark about 5ft long. We then had to stop fishing as the sharks had gone into a feeding frenzy and it was becoming quite scary because we had to row back to our boat later in our small dinghy.

Next morning at first light the three boats started to up anchor. Unfortunately, our anchor chain was well and truly snagged around some coral head, no matter how I tried it would not budge. The anchor was 40 ft down and the only way to retrieve it was to don my tanks, which I did. On the way down I had never been so nervous in my life on a dive, thinking about last night's shark experience, however I could not afford to lose my anchor in such a remote place. So, with grit and determination, I managed with great relief to untangle the mess.

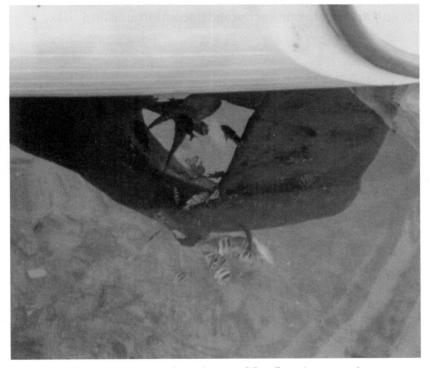

The water is so clear it was like floating on air.

When we eventually left the wind was getting stronger, gusting up to 25 knots, so we had no choice but to put to sea with no alternative shelter. After that we had two of our toughest days at sea for a long time, on our way to Tahiti. Punching into steep seas that jarred the boat every few minutes creating major problems just to make a cup of tea. Then, with only 60 miles to go, a huge wave hit the side of the boat with tremendous force and broke the auxiliary rudder off our self-steering gear. It was too difficult to retrieve and was broken in half anyway, so we let it go. On reaching Tahiti we had to order a new one.

Disaster when the self steering rudder broke off.

Sailing in French Polynesia

Arriving at 3.30 a.m on a pitch-dark night with squall after squall chasing us along we were very glad to drop anchor in Papeete's sheltered harbour and have our first real night's rest for three days. On the Sunday morning, we went to church to listen to the wonderful choirs they have. As I looked out of the window Gringo was perfectly framed by it. The sun was shining through the palms and the sweet music of the choir singing. I really felt at peace and knew I was in the South Pacific, it could be nowhere else.

Tahiti is such a beautiful island. Sadie described it well when she said, "Its like driving through one huge botanical garden". We hired a car to see the sights. Unfortunately, the island's economy is in a mess, they have priced themselves out of the market. All the hotels we visited seemed to be only about a quarter full. During our three week stay they had three strikes and several demonstrations. The cost of living is astronomical with a loaf of bread costing $4. I really don't know how these gentle people make ends meet.

What a wonderful 11th wedding anniversary.

The market place is a blaze of colour with many species of flowers and every type of vegetable imaginable. An interesting thing we bought was a coconut crab with huge powerful pincers taped up with masking tape to protect stray fingers. I don't think the flavour was as good as lobster though. The majority of the meat is in the claws as the tail is not edible and the meat has a slightly earthy taste.

Whilst in Tahiti we had the pleasure of celebrating our 11th wedding anniversary. We dined royally at a local hotel and were presented with leis of flowers by the beautiful Tahitian girls that had entertained us so well with their traditional dance to the incredible rhythms of Polynesian type drums. All in all we had a truly memorable anniversary.

From Tahiti, I had to organise a new self-steering rudder to be sent out. On phoning the suppliers, Pumpkin Marine in London, I was informed that they wanted £880 to fly it out of which they said half was for freight. As the unit was only 10 months old I wasn't at all pleased about this. So, after wasting well over $100 on phone calls and being told "it was probably hit by a fish" and "you had too much sail up", I gave up on them and phoned the manufactures in Germany who were very efficient. They agreed it should not have broken. They offered a new part free of charge so I agreed to pay the freight, at a total cost of £200 as against £450 freight that Pumpkin Marine quoted. Within a week the part arrived via Air France, to our great relief.

When I went to collect it from the airport all the handlers were on strike and riots were taking place there. I managed to get through the crowd, but the man at the depot refused to hand over anything, even though I tried to explain I was desperate and needed it to carry on sailing. Walking away feeling more than a little angry I walked past the storage sheds. I could not believe my eyes. There lying amongst loads of packages was my new rudder. Without a second thought I just picked it up and carried on walking. It was not a small thing, with the shaft and rudder, it was over 6ft long and heavy too. I just carried on walking through all the rioting. Sometimes to make things happen, you have to push your luck a little.

Once back on the boat and with the steering rudder fitted we were able to continue on our way to Moorea, after three weeks rest in Tahiti. Arriving in the lovely fjord like, tranquil anchorage of Cook's Bay on Moorea we felt pleased to be out of the busy town of Papeete, with its roar of traffic. There appears to be a few islands in this group, all very similar to each other, such as Raiatea, Tahaa, Huahine, all with unusual names. A village in Tahaa takes the biscuit for strange names with Faaaha, and, yes, that is spelt right. Try saying that after a few beers.

We seemed to fall in love with all of them especially Raiatea, with its delightful little town of Uturoa. We had the distinction of being the first yacht to enter their new little marina that had not yet been opened officially. From the East coast of Raiatea Polynesian sailors made repeated passages to New Zealand and Hawaii to colonise them.

Both were over 2,000 miles away, besides other voyages over vast stretches of the Pacific, with no compass or sextant - using only the stars and wind. The feats of Raiatean seamanship stand above all others and makes what we are doing look like child's play. We visited the Marea Taputapuatea that is said to have been the holiest place in the whole of Polynesia, where sacrifices and prayers were offered up for departing sailors before their truly incredible voyages into the virtually unknown world. Having crossed a few oceans myself now, I take my hat off to them.

Many of the strange alters we came across

On reaching Bora Bora which is reputedly the world's most beautiful island, we were greeted by our old friends on the yacht "Finback" whom we had last seen back in the Galapagos, where we celebrated James' birthday at a little dockside restaurant "Sombrella". What better excuse for another celebration did we need!! Whilst in Bora Bora a group of us decided to climb the 2,000 ft high mountain.

At 8 a.m five of us tramped off from the yacht club towards the foot of the mountain. Four hours later we reached its pointed top and to our amazement found three Frenchmen up there waiting for a helicopter to pick them up from its peak, which measured about 12 sq.ft. We were duly asked to squat down over the edge whilst the helicopter hovered for the pick-up. It turned out to be one of the scariest moments of my life, clinging on for dear life with a tremendous down draught from the huge rotor blades a few feet above our heads tugging at our bodies as we tenaciously gripped on. Unfortunately for the three French men all did not go according to plan as the pilot had to make a quick getaway, leaving two behind due to strong winds. He refused to come back for a second attempt, much to our relief.

We arrived back down to our respective boats 8 hours later after setting off feeling more than a little tired, but well satisfied with our ambitious conquering of the famous landmark that can be seen from so many miles out to sea. It is also featured in films and photos of the South Pacific. Bora Bora is a meeting place for almost all the sailors crossing the Pacific, as a stop off point before the next leg to either Samoa or the Cook Islands, and its visitors are truly international.

Every one of its 2,000 inhabitants seemed occupied in celebrations of some sort or other. Some people say it's the Bastille Day celebrations but I doubt if half the people know what that was. Even so, the parades, singing and dancing were a sight not to be missed in ones life time and seemed to go on for weeks until everyone gets fed up with all the entertainment. The colourful costumes, harmonic music, incredible dance routines, huge floats decorated with lush greenery and gloriously colourful flowers, entice the visitor into taking part and mingling with these friendly people and catching the infectious fun.

On the 25th July, we finally tore ourselves away from Bora Bora bound for Maupiti, a month behind our original schedule. Maupiti turned out to be a miniature Bora Bora, an absolute gem of a place. We stocked up with fruit of all kinds that grow in abundance on this island, including the sought after 'pamplemousse', a fruit similar to a grapefruit but sweeter and twice as big.

During our second evening we saw the brightest meteorite we have ever seen during a beach barbecue. It lit the whole sky up like a great rocket of white light. It was so close the red hot remains could be clearly seen falling to earth as it burnt out.

Suvarrov and Dengue Fever

We left Maupiti Monday morning 29th July in clear blue skies and flat seas feeling more than a little concerned at the prospect of being becalmed for the 650-mile trip to Suvarrov or Suvarrwarrow. No one seems to know the real name, even the British Admiralty call it by either name. Anyhow, becalmed we were definitely not After about 4 hours a breeze sprang up out of the South that got stronger and stronger until it reached 25 to 30 knots, which continued for the next three days, giving us a very unpleasant ride indeed. A huge swell came up from the South and the wind backed to the East creating a very confused sea. The one good thing was that we made good speed, holding 6 knots day and night. On the third day out we were treated to that rare spectacle the "green flash" as the sun went down. We later discovered it was witnessed by other boats the same night. So alas it was not a figment of the imagination.

The only "Kids on the Block" with just ten people inhabiting the Island.

After five days, we arrived in Suvarrov to a wonderful welcome from the local family, who inhabited the island. Our checking in procedure was done sitting under a tree drinking from coconuts that a young lad had shimmed up a tree to get for us. You can't get fresher than that! In the evening a banquet was laid on for us, consisting of fresh fish and coconut cooked several ways.

We only intended to spend a couple of nights there but ended up staying a week due to mainly the incredible diving. In one area of the lagoon a group of gentle manta rays lived and were so tame it was possible to dive down and stroke them. It was quite a thrill to touch the huge gentle delta winged monsters. They didn't seem to show any fear and gently swam around us with their slow motion flying action. To me it was one of the highlights of my life.

The next stage of the trip turned out to be a real nightmare. After saying our goodbyes we set off bound for American Samoa, a distance of some 450 miles. After about two hours I was struck down by a real blinding headache that got progressively worse as the day went by. It then turned into a high fever with pains in the kidneys and limbs. Within a few hours I had difficulty in standing up. Sadie proved to be a real-life saver. She sailed the boat virtually single handed for the rest of the trip and took care of me.

On the second day another worry added to an already difficult situation. Vicky's temperature shot up to 103.8 degrees F. So now two of us were down with the mystery virus. Fortunately, Vicky improved after a couple of days, but I got progressively worse. We were told it could be dengue fever by a doctor who was in radio contact on another yacht. On reaching American Samoa Sadie radioed ahead and an ambulance whisked us away to the local hospital where dengue fever was confirmed.

The fact that over 80 people had already died of Dengue Fever in the Cook Islands didn't make the situation much brighter. The doctor told Sadie that the platelets in my blood had dropped and none were available for transfusion. When the platelets drop low enough a knock or a cut could cause you to bleed to death. Things seemed to be going from bad to worse.

Being in the President Lyndon Johnson Hospital in Samoa was not part of my travel plans. I hate being ill at the best of times, but this hospital was something else. The poor chap in the bed next to me died in the night and was left there till the next morning. At least he was quiet, which was more than can be said for the fellow on the other side of me. A huge man who snored and grunted and farted like you would not believe. All night needless to say sleep did not come easy to me.

The next morning Sadie came to see me along with a good sailing friends Denis and Cam Raedeke. "You need to get yourself out of here buddy",he said, "People are dying here" as one more body was being carried out.

By the afternoon I was booked on a flight to Hawaii with Cam and Sadie. I was transported to the Straub Hospital where I spent three long days in intensive care. I didn't know until later that twice Sadie had been told to prepare herself for the worst as most people die from Dengue fever. Fortunately, I was very fit and I am sure that helped.

As for Vicky and James, friends on "Skyeboat" had volunteered to look after them in American Samoa. Unbeknown to us all the yachts arriving from the Cook Islands were put in quarantine to contain the epidemic. No one was allowed ashore for three days.

Anyway, to cut a long story short I survived the fever that lasted seven days and after another two weeks rest I was back to normal, apart from the stone in weight loss.

Samoa is one big tropical garden.

From American Samoa, we sailed overnight to Western Samoa. A visit to the famous Aggie Greys Hotel was a real treat here. The tables groaned under the weight of food dished up and the singing and dancing were superb. Western Samoa is a must for any traveller in this part of the world. A walk up to Robert Louis Stevenson's grave on the mountain top of Apia must be one of the prettiest walks anywhere in the world. There were trees and shrubs beyond description. Stevenson's monument carries his immortal words so appropriate to the cruising sailor:-

> Under the wide and starry sky,
> Dig my grave and let me lie.
> Glad did I live and gladly die,
> And I laid me down with a will.
> This be the last verse you gave for me;
> Here he lies where he longed to be.
> Home is the sailor, home from sea,
> And the hunter from the hill.

In Western Samoa we discovered that, at some time in the past during German rule there, quite a few teak trees were planted. Now the benefits are being reaped with the availability of teak at unbelievably low prices. I bought enough to build new seats and a table around the stern of the boat. A total of 144ft for just $20. In Europe, it would have cost 20 times that.

On the 4th September we sailed out of Apia harbour, bound for Vava'u, but on rounding the West of the island found the wind dead on the nose. So we altered course for Niuetoputapa to break the journey and give us a better slant on the wind and where we could wait until it backed to the East hopefully.
Niuatoputapu turned out to be a very poverty-stricken island but very interesting. Pigs, dogs and people all lived under the same roof here in perfect harmony. While we were there everyone was busy tidying up the village ready for the annual visit from the King. Unfortunately, we later found out the King couldn't make it due to health reasons. It must have been a real disappointment for them after all the preparations. They made a 50x3 metre tapa cloth for him to walk on. It took many months to make.
We found them to be the usual friendly South Pacific people, always eager to please. One night they took us night fishing though I'm sure we were only in the way. We were never treated anything less than equals. During our long trek through the dense jungle and along rocky beaches I noticed them picking up hermit crabs about the size of golf balls. On reaching the desired spot for fishing we had to wait an hour or so for the tide to drop a little more. A fire was lit on the beach from coconut husks and drift wood. They all emptied their

bulging pocket of hermit crabs and proceeded to cook them on the fire - cooked until they emerged from their shells and then until they turned nut brown. The fishermen then proceeded to eat them like kids eating sweets. As guests we were handed the first ones. After being told they were very good to eat we apprehensively nibbled and pretended to enjoy them, but I could manage without them.

The following day we had an invitation to a Tongan feast. The only problem with that is it turned out to be a little too authentic. There were sea slugs, sea snails, sea weed and tiny suckling pigs, which we were all expected to heartily tuck into. It was the one and only time that Sadie didn't have to work hard at sticking to her diet. It was a real experience and we suffered no after effects, which is more than can be said about some of the hotels we have stayed in. Our plates were banana leaves and our knives and forks were our fingers. As we ate, dozens of people gathered outside, all peering in wanting to take a closer look at our fair skin and blonde hair but all in a light-hearted and fascinated manner.

Gringo making up for lost time.

A storm to Tonga

When the time came to leave I checked a weather fax print out on the yacht "Lazy Rebel" to see it was giving a wind from the North East, ideal for our trip to Tonga. So off we set and all ran to true form making the first seventy miles in good time along with three other yachts. At 10 o'clock at night, Sadie called me up to say she could see an island off our starboard side. At first I said it was impossible but then on looking myself I wasn't so sure. I even checked our course with our main compass. I also consulted the charts again but no island should have been there. Within a short time I was to find out what it was in no uncertain terms. The wind was coming from the N.E. and the thick black bank of cloud which we'd now established was downwind of us, so I thought it would move away from us. While pondering these thoughts and still sailing nicely in about 15 knots of wind still from the N.E. a gust of wind hit us with such ferocity from the South no less as to almost knock us over. I immediately let go of the sheets and then went on deck to drop some sail. By this time, we were being lashed by torrential rain like I have never seen before. It was difficult to breathe in it and the wind by now was screaming in the rigging. With the sheets and halyards freed it was still impossible to get the sails down due to the wind pressure on them.

Sadie started the engine to try and get the nose into the wind. I was convinced at this stage we had at least lost two sails due to the flogging. The clew of the head sail was whip cracking like a machine gun. The wind by now was impossible to stand up in, its force was so great. With the engine revving hard to bring us up to windward and me clinging on for dear life to the mast, I managed to pull the main sail down, but the normal bungies that are used to stow the sail were a waste of time as they couldn't hold the sail to the boom in such wind strength. In the end I got my hands on a mooring rope and lashed it down with that. In all it took the best part of an hour to lash everything down and get all the sails under control. By the time I returned to the welcome warmth of the cabin I was cold, wet and exhausted. I couldn't believe that James slept all the way through it.

In all the miles of sailing we've done it's the first time we've had to lie a hull, which we did for 12 hours. We later learned that the other boats that left with us had worse problems than us. "Lazy Rebel" suffered a knock down and "Adelante" had a head sail torn to shreds and several stanchions bent over due to the weight of water hitting the spray dodgers. "Tin" had so much water over the decks it found its way down the breather pipe to the diesel tanks and put his engine out of action for a while. The wind at its peak reached 71 knots according to the other boats in the area. I couldn't estimate its speed as I'd never been in such wind strength before and our wind speed meter had broken.

All I know is that I'm amazed that Gringo came out of it unscathed apart from a little stitching in the main and mizzen sails coming adrift. It took us two days and nights to reach the island of Vava'u in the Kingdom of Tonga, a distance of some 160 miles.

One of the regular celebrations with the King of Tonga

Tonga turned out to be a real delight. The Vava'u group is a real yachtsman's dream with numerous fjord like inlets that are completely surrounded by one massive reef. Once inside the reef weeks could be spent exploring the many islands in the wonderfully calm waters. While passing between two islands we were treated to a fantastic display by a huge humpback whale rolling over on his back and smacking his massive fins on the water. It was a sight never to be forgotten. We managed to get about 50 feet from him viewing the display for about 20 minutes. After he had dived down into the deep clear blue water I bitterly regretted not putting on my mask and snorkel and going in the water with him. It was an opportunity we'll probably never get again being in sheltered warm waters.

Spinaker Flying in Tonga

One very interesting place we visited was Mariners Cave that can only be entered by diving down and swimming underwater for about 15 feet and eventually coming up into the darkness of the cave. Once your eyes attune to the light, that only enters through the blue of the water, it's quite a spectacle as the ever-changing pressures create a mist one-second and clear visibility the next, along with the constant popping of ears.

Whilst anchored one night in one of the outer islands we very nearly lost our friend Peter off the boat "Lazy Rebel". He had been for a drink with another friend Mani off "Adelante", when the weather took a turn for the worse and a strong off shore wind picked up. Peter decided to row back to his boat and make sure all was well. He got into his dinghy in the pitch-black night and cast off only to realise to his horror one of the oars had gone. Within minutes he was swept out to sea. Mani heard him shout but by the time he had started the engine and got the anchor up on"Adelante", Peter was nowhere to be seen or heard. Mani who is an experienced seaman decided to motor downwind intending to go well past where he thought Peter could have reached and then start a zig zag search pattern upwind to try and locate Peter. It was like looking for a needle in a haystack. Unbelievably on his first transit he heard Peter's voice in the dark. Mani had gone at least a quarter of a mile past where he thought the dinghy could have blown to and wasn't expecting to find Peter that far out. It just went to prove how fast a dinghy can be blown out to sea. Peter was a very lucky man that night.

Our time in Tonga passed by all too quickly. We met the King and Crown Prince at the agricultural show one day, diving the next, visiting uninhabited islands the next, so it was almost a rest when we checked out of Nafu and put to sea again.

Fiji

Our 450 mile trip to Fiji was one of our best yet, with a steady 15-20 knots of wind just aft of the beam that held steady for the duration of the trip. The only problem was that we made better time than planned and it caused us to arrive at night. Suva is a tricky entrance but we didn't fancy having to hove to all night so we edged our way in the dark. Fiji would be our last group of South Pacific Islands before New Zealand, so it would be here we would make our preparations for our long haul South.

Suva, the main city of Fiji, is a cosmopolitan, bustling trading centre with a mixture of Asian, Chinese, Indian and Fijian people, all plying their trade and competing against fellow traders to sell you the best bargain. The old Royal Suva Yatch Club still thrives and maintains its air of colonialism with breakfast, lunch and dinner served on the lawn, if you want it, in a relaxed and happy atmosphere. It bears its Royal name with fierce pride. Long may it continue in its present mode.

Fiji is a great place to get any jobs done on the boat. Gringo's seat covers were starting to get a bit worse for wear. I made a few enquiries and found a shop that recovered chairs etc. I went in and inquired and was told no problem, we'll come down to the boat and measure up for you. He told us to choose a material, which we did, a really good quality heavy draylon that would be practical and hard wearing. He later came down to Gringo and after a quick calculation said it would be £60. I wasn't sure whether he meant £60 per hour or £60 for the material. That will cover everything he said to my amazement. "Are you sure?" I said. He then apologised that it would have been cheaper but the men will have to be paid overtime to get it done on time. In two days, we had a complete new set of seats for Gringo and a fantastic job. I'm sure there will never again be such a bargain job done on my boat.

One criticism of Fiji is the hopelessly outdated and drawn out checking in and out procedure that wasted a day each way, with enough form filling to give a reporter writer's cramp. The team of bureaucrats would be better employed in maintaining the navigation lights in the area. During a two week stay in Suva no less than five yachts came to grief on the approaching reefs. If only a few more beacons could be employed along the outer reefs this dreadful toll could be avoided.

The strange tasting Kava Roots. Always had to be given to the Village Chief as a present.

We purchased our, almost compulsory, Kava from the market before leaving Suva to hand out as gifts to the village chiefs. The first batch was handed to one of the chiefs on the island of Beqa pronounced by the locals as Mbenga. Kava is a very mild narcotic that gives a slight tingle to your lips and tongue and tastes like dishwater. After three cups at our first Kava ceremony no after effects could be felt. It is all a very serious affair carried out in careful ritual acts between the chief, head man and guests. This form of greeting has been handed down for generations and is used widely throughout Tonga, Samoa and Fiji.

After a couple of day hops along the South coast of Fiji we worked our way in through the reefs to Musket Cove, home to the famous Musket Cove Yacht Club where we became lifelong members. After a trip up through the Yaswara Islands where we visited some of the uninhabited islands, we thought it time to sail back to Lautoka to check out as the cyclone season was fast creeping up on us. On our way back down through the islands we spent a night at the island of Waya where we went ashore to present the chief with the customary Kava.

One always tends to think of village chiefs as simple fishermen or farmers, but in many cases they turn out to be very intellectual men.

The chief of Waya for instance had been educated at Oxford and the London School of Economics and turned out to be a very interesting man, a King of his little island and highly respected by all the villagers, one whose word is law.

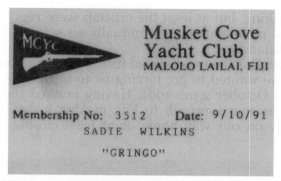

Musket Cove
Yacht Club
MALOLO LAILAI, FIJI

Membership No: 3512   Date: 9/10/91
SADIE   WILKINS

"GRINGO"

Mixing with the Locals on the Islands off the coast of Fiji.

New Zealand here we come

We wasted the best part of the day checking out with the inevitable pile of form filling, but at least the officials were very friendly. After refuelling and provisioning we eventually set sail on the 1,100-mile leg to New Zealand.

On leaving the pass the wind played its tricks on us, blowing straight from where we wanted to go, forcing us to bear away to the West. The date was October 23rd, 1991. Having crossed the longitude of 180 degrees on our approach to Fiji, making a day disappear, we were officially on our way home or at least closing the longitude anyway.

Barnacles had to be scraped off with a Spade.

We arrived on a fresh spring day, the last day in October. What a relief it was as the motion of the boat stopped, after eight boisterous days at sea, the Bay of Islands immediately captured us with its rich green fertile land and placid little anchorages. Pulling up into Opua we moored alongside an English boat and out popped our friend

David Saddler, who said "Welcome to New Zealand, congratulations, do have a sherry". What a very English welcome!

In New Zealand, the customs are very strict and any foodstuffs are vetted in case of contamination. One of the things you can't bring in is flour. When the customs officer boarded us he was very polite but he had to confiscate ours. Instead of carrying the whole bag away he decided it had to be tipped into a black plastic bag so he stood on deck trying to transfer the flour from bag to bag. It was like a comic routine with the breeze and the slight roll of the boat, coupled with the fact he did not have his sea legs and the flour went everywhere, all over the boat, all over him, and when he eventually left the boat, he left a flour trail along the dock. Why he didn't put the original bag into the black sack whole I will never know!!

One of the many unspoilt places in New Zealand.

This was to be our home for the next six months. We felt like kids with a new toy. All this beautiful country stretched out before us waiting to be explored.

During our time, We met up with old friends Tony and Cherry Hopkins, who we had last seen three years ago in Antigua. They showed us the way around Auckland and took us to the car auctions where we purchased an old Honda Accord. How well the old car served us, clocking up almost 15,000 kms in our five and a half months of ownership, and we never had a problem with it.

New Zealand is a land of breath-taking scenery from top to bottom. Especially the South Island where the contrasts are incredible with rolling meadows, dense pine forest, sub-tropical forests, alpine mountains, volcanos and oh those beautiful lakes, hot bubbling springs, old out-back towns to modern high-rise cities. What a fabulous time we had touring this great country.

All dressed up in borrowed clothes to go and see Placid Domingo

An interesting thing happened to us in Auckland. We decided to go and see Placido Domingo who was giving an open-air concert at Western Springs. Before the concert we went for a meal with the orchestra, as we had managed to get two limited tickets for this pre-show event. At the meal, we joined a middle-aged couple with whom we got on very well. It wasn't until about half an hour had passed and a man came to the table and said, "good evening Prime Minister, so glad you could make it". The Prime Minister replied "good evening Sir Mills, this is Denis and Sadie Wilkins. Denis and Sadie, have you met Sir Les Mills - Mayor of Auckland"!!! Later that evening Jim Bolger, the Prime Minister and his wife, Joan, wanted to know all about our trip and what it was like cruising with children. Before leaving he signed a card and gave it to us telling us to drop in anytime we were in Wellington. Never in our lives had we felt so important. Incidentally the concert was fantastic with Placido Domingo singing to more than 60,000 people who gave him numerous ovations. A night I don't think we will forget in a hurry.

The letter the Prime Minister Jim Bolger wrote to us.

We made so many good friends in New Zealand. Even the children enjoyed their time going to school for a couple of months and meeting up with children their age. We kept Gringo in Gulf Harbour Marina which was convenient for Auckland and getting all the jobs done.

One day walking along the breakwater of Gulf Harbour with James, we spotted the biggest octopus we had ever seen in the waters edge. Stupidly I decided I was going to catch it and climbed down the huge boulders quietly towards it. When I got close to it, it must have been over 3 ft. across, I gently put my hand in the water and grabbed hold of a tentacle thinking I was going to pull it out and throw it up on the rocks of the breakwater. However, he had other ideas, clamped himself to the rocks and started pulling me in the opposite direction. Immediately panic set in for both of us. I could not believe the strength of it. All I wanted to do was let go, but his suckers were starting to get a grip on my arm. With an almighty wrench I got my arm free and quickly scrambled up the rocks with my heart rate soaring. James wanted to know why I didn't pull him out. I felt such a fool. I thought I was going to eat him and he thought he was going to eat me. From now on I steer clear of large octopuses.

Austrailia here we come

It became more and more difficult to tear ourselves away but winter drew on so I knew we must. All the jobs we could find had been done on the boat and she looked in pristine condition. On Thursday, April 23rd, having stocked up the boat and said our goodbyes, we pushed on gently out of Opua, Bay of Islands bound for Bundaberg, Australia - 1,300 miles away. A trip that no yachtsman ever looks forward to as the Tasman Sea can be a very nasty stretch of water indeed as depressions come up very quickly from the South and sometimes give gale force winds on the nose, or worse still cyclones can track down from the North so it is crucial to get the timing right.

With our new bottom paint on the boat she slipped through the water better than ever, clocking up 156 miles in 24 hours on our second day out and that was with half a knot adverse current. Our third night out the Tasman lived up to its reputation with boisterous seas and 30 knot winds.

This was something we did not enjoy one little bit as our stomachs and limbs had become weak due to six months of marina life. That day neither Sadie nor myself hardly ate anything, but the kids had their usual ravenous appetites, which didn't help our situation at all. To make life worse the wind backed until it came around onto the nose forcing us to sail South of our course for 12 hours. On the Sunday evening we broke through the magic door and into a high-pressure zone, even though there was 100% cloud cover.

The air became warmer and the wind eased up to a gentle breeze from the South, enabling us to resume our course for the next few days. For the following few days the wind stayed light forcing us either to motor or wallow around in the middle of the Tasman, so motoring it was to be. On our sixth day out we sailed all day under cruising chute, main and mizzen, making good speed and feeling very happy with ourselves and our progress.

However, all good things come to an end and the following day the wind died again. What was worse we received the news that a late cyclone was forming 1,000 miles to the north of us, travelling our way at 10 knots. Having lost a friend in a cyclone when the yacht "Flying Cloud" went down did nothing to ease our nerves. I found myself going over and over the charts calculating our position and the past track of cyclones. I spent the late hours of the night studying weather print outs. I decided to alter course to Brisbane, even though it is only 70 miles nearer. That could be enough to get safely in port if it carried on our way and gained momentum. The only thing we could do is push on and keep everything crossed. The normal track is for cyclones to veer South then South East in the southern hemisphere. They travel along like a huge snake causing havoc to all in their unpredictable path. We spent the next two days in sheer agony trying to decide will it go straight, will it swing this way or that way, will we manage to outrun it. On Thursday night we picked up on the radio that cyclone Innis was starting to swing S.S.W. Once on that course it would more than likely stay on it until it died out, which meant that it would pass well to the East of us. Needless to say we breathed a great sigh of relief and returned to the more usual happy atmosphere on Gringo.

Over this trip most nights we had electrical storms. On the later part of this trip it caused a little concern because looking up from the deck our two alloy masts would make perfect lightning conductors. With first thoughts of being blown away and then the thought of being fried, this hadn't been the easiest of trips.

After our two days of torment that fortunately amounted to nothing more than a lack of wind for us, cyclone Innis fizzled out much to the relief of all the yachties within a thousand-mile radius. The following days to Brisbane saw us bounding along in fresh trade winds and clear blue skies to reach our port in 9 1/2 days, not bad going to cover 1,300 miles.

We crossed the tricky sand banks of Morton Bay and entered the Brisbane River as darkness fell, straining our eyes to pick up the navigation lights against the incandescent glow of a million city lights. We edged our way up the river until we were safely docked at the customs berth. The Australian customs men turned out to be very friendly in spite of their fearsome reputation. Soon after our old friend, Ronnie Robilliard from Guernsey, who had been keeping track of us, came down to welcome us to Australia with a huge bag of jumbo prawns, fresh bread and butter, that we quickly devoured before getting our heads down for a much needed night's sleep. The following morning, we moved on up the river to moor off the botanical gardens right in the heart of the city, with its massive skyscrapers along the water's edge. It seemed a completely alien world to the one we had become used to, but exciting none-the-less. We enjoyed our time in the bustling get up and go city, but after five days we thought of the blue waters further north and decided to start moving on, arriving late at night at Mooloolaba.

The following day we started walking from the marina to the town and within a few minutes a car pulled up and the driver called out our names much to our surprise. It was Betty and David off the yacht "Zingara", who we had last seen on a remote island beach in the Yasawa Islands. What a small world it is and it seemed even smaller when they took us to the little marina they were in, as they had been hauled out near some old friends of ours on the yacht "Tangara 111", whom we first befriended in Porto Santo on the other side of the world. Working our way north we took the channel behind Fraser Island, the largest sand island in the world. The wild dingos there follow visitors around in the hope of picking up scraps of food. They all look as if they need it pretty badly but apparently it is the way they are supposed to look. Fraser Island has some good wildlife with its dingos and cockatoos flying around, but unfortunately for us the weather turned foul and we had rain for three solid days, thus encouraging us to push on to Bundaberg. Notable for its huge sugar cane fields and rum factory that permeates the air with the smell of rum in the whole area.

The locals charming the visitors.

Whilst in Bunderburg we purchased four plastic jerry cans to carry extra emergency water supplies. I knew that with the Indian Ocean and the Red Sea ahead water may be difficult to obtain, so the thing to do was take on as much as possible whenever we could. It wasn't until later that I tasted the stored water from the cans and found the water to have a very strong rum flavour! The cans had obviously been used for storage at the Bunderburg Rum Factory in a previous life. Every cup of tea tasted as if a shot of rum had been added - a real bonus.

After another few days of miserable weather we decided to do something about it and get further North to the Equator and warmer weather. So off we set to sea again for a couple of days and eventually put into Pearl Bay. Hey presto, we burst through into glorious sunshine and blue sea.

After a day of swimming and shell collecting on the beach we set off the next morning on a flat calm sea but in thick fog, confident that it would burn away when the sun strengthened, which proved so in an hour. A calm on the Barrier Reef is a real calm, the sea resembling a smooth mirror with the absence of the more usual ocean swell. By the same token because it is so shallow a steep choppy sea quickly comes up when the wind rises. If the outer reef were not there this would be a very inhospitable coast to seafarers.

The fine white sand of Whitsunday Beach.

We sailed through the Whitsunday passage on the 4th June exactly 222 years to the day that my great hero Captain James Cook came through the same stretch of water. Most of the Whitsunday's are uninhabited to this day and I can't believe that it has changed much over the years. The islands that have been developed have been done so very tastefully to cater for the upper-class holiday maker but unfortunately for us a few of them actively discourage yachts from landing on their hallowed beaches. If a few of the resort islands discourage yachts quite the opposite could be said of the sleepy little outback town of Bowen. The cruising club there go out of their way to make all the yachties welcome, as did the harbour staff.

How many port control officers get their car out and bring you back to your boat after paying your dues? Also the supermarket staff gave us a lift back after provisioning. Bowen seems to have got left behind with development but to have retained a good old fashioned courtesy, so sadly missing in many societies today.

Horses cooling down after a five mile treck on Magnetic Island.

Moving ever North on leaving Bowen we cruised in company with ex-Olympic and one-ton world champion sailor from New Zealand Chris Buzade and his family for a few days. We had previously befriended them in Fiji and enjoyed our reunion again over a few beers and yarns.

Our next port of call turned out to be one of the best islands in the Barrier Reef in our opinion; that was Magnetic Island. Magnetic by name and by nature. A place very reminiscent of some of the West Indian Islands, but a little better run. One of the highlights there was the horse riding on the beach. You could let the horses go at full pelt and then take them for a cooling swim in the sea. The horses seemed to enjoy every minute frolicking around in the water and some were

Our hero Captain James Cook with another James at his feet

quite reluctant to come out. There can be no better way to see the Australian bush than on horse-back. Even though we only had a five-mile trek, it was enough to get the feel and the smell of the countryside.

From Magnetic Island north, we visited some of the resort islands until reaching the main town of northern Queensland - Cairns. A town geared up well to tourism with great wave piercing catamarans taking visitors by the hundreds out to the Barrier Reef. A town with lots of up market shops mainly owned by the Japanese selling opals, leather gear and fine clothes. If the tourist looks a little farther inland of Cairns there is so much more on offer with the beautiful Atherton Tablelands and rainforests. Perhaps it is better that the majority of visitors stick to the bright lights of the city.

The Kuranda Railway was like stepping back in time.

One trip that we did go on that is a must for any visitor to Cairns is a trip on the Kuranda railway. The train winds its way up through the sugar cane fields and into the mountains to the little village of Kuranda where the market operates daily with great success selling anything from jars of honey to boomerangs.

During our visit to Atherton we spent a few days driving a little further into the bush. We drove along mile upon mile of dry red dusty roads winding their endless route through the parched gum trees with the occasional kangaroo lying dead on the roadside. At times there would be countless termite hills, often two or three meters high, monuments to the little creatures graft and perseverance.

Atherton Tableland is totally different to the bush-lands with lush green forests and numerous lakes. We stayed at a hotel near Lake Tinaroo that must have been as near to paradise as it is possible to get. Overlooking the lake with Bougainvilleas growing in great profusion all around, what a place to wake up to in the morning; I'm sure one could never tire of the beauty of the place.

One of the many termite hills that abound Australia

Moving on from Cairns to Cooktown stopping at Port Douglas and Hope Island. Hope Islands very nearly changed the course of history. When Captain Cook saw it ahead in 1770 he turned out to sea to avoid it as the light was fading and he didn't want to get involved with islands and reefs after dark. It turned out to be a decision he bitterly regretted as a couple of hours later, in the dark, the Endeavour struck a reef that now bears the name of his ship. After three days and the jettisoning of 50 tons of ballast and 6 cannons, the Endeavour was re-floated and eventually brought to rest in what is now called Cook Town, where repairs took 48 days to carry out.

Had the Endeavour not been re-floated and successfully sailed back to England, Australians would now most probably have been speaking French as they were hot on Cook's heels and trying to expand their Pacific colonies.

In the entrance of the Endeavour River approaching Cooktown our travelling companions Keith and Carol, aboard their yacht "Kirsten Jayne" ironically nearly lost their boat. In 25 knots of wind they made their approach picking up and following the leading beacons. Keith started his engine and began to take down the head sail when the lazy sheet went over the side and snagged around the propeller. Having already stowed and put covers on the mainsail, it was impossible to get any sail up in time and, with the wind strength, it would have been almost impossible to sail away from the fast approaching lee shore. Fortunately, we were not too far behind and chased after them at full speed.

By the time we reached them we were in two and a half meters of water with waves starting to break all around us. The boats were tossing wildly and the first attempt to get a line across failed. We had to make one more approach, if this had failed we couldn't have made another run in as it was already dangerously shallow for us and to go aground in the sea that was running would have meant disaster. The seas would have soon smashed the two boats to pulp. The second approach I made nose first on the windward side to try to give a little shelter. As soon as a line was tossed across to Sadie, I gave full power astern to keep safe distance between the two boats and to pull us into deeper water. We then turned the boat around and Sadie attached the line to the stern and we started the haul back to the main channel against the strong head winds. When we made the first line fast on to Gringo our keels could only have been inches from the bottom.

Needless to say as we clawed our way into deeper water and eventually into the safety of Cooktown we all breathed a sigh of relief - especially Keith and Carol. That night we celebrated with a meal ashore at the local hotel as a thank-you from "Kirsten Jayne".

Poor Keith's troubles were not over yet as the rope around the prop had pulled the engine off the mountings and bent the 'p' bracket [the second time in six months]. Keith had the unenviable task of diving underneath his boat with a hydraulic jack in hand to straighten the bracket while I had the better job of standing on guard looking out for crocodiles. With jacks, blocks, and levers the job was eventually carried out after 10 dives.

The trade winds from Cairns to Cape York once established, blow with remarkable regularity and force. Quite often holding 25 knots plus for days on end, making passages quick, but often bumpy, with the short steep chop of the shallow water inside the Barrier Reef. In these winds, we made good time from Cooktown to Cape Flattery from where millions of tons of silica sand is mined from its pure white coastline.

From Cape Flattery our next stop was Lizard Island, the most northerly of the resort islands. What a pleasant surprise we had there when the cruise liner "Reef Escape'" pulled in. We had a call from its Captain with an invitation to join him for dinner that evening. A little bewildered as to why at first, we later learned the Captain was a keen sailor and was interested in looking over our boat and to hear an account of our journey. We ended up as guests of honour at his table and our story was put to good use entertaining the passengers. He even let us use one of the spare cabins where the kids had a bath!! Sadie just let the water run over her hair to give it a good rinse from the accumulation of salt water. After a year of saving water, it was heaven. Even a proper flushing toilet, no pumping!!

Lizard Island was the type of place we pulled into intending to spend a couple of days there and ending up spending over a week. We became good friends with the people who run the research station and ended up with a full social programme there. Diving in the day at the incredible cod hole where giant potato cod around 500lb in weight are so tame you can feed them by hand and stroke them.

There is also a giant moray eel who has become accustomed to being handled by divers and appears to enjoy every minute of it. Even Sadie found the courage to pat him gently and tickle under his chin. The massive cod down there are so clumsy that quite often they bump against you whilst swimming past giving you a gentle nudge. In the evening we had a BBQ at the research station along with the staff of the resort while the kids played cricket on the beach. All in all we had some pretty good times at Lizard Island but the next leg of our trip looked like being a bit lonely as towns north of Lizard are non existent until Gove.

Day after day we pushed North from one anchorage to another. Sometimes as little as twenty miles, sometimes seventy, all the time with very little sign of human life, apart from the odd lonely fishing boat trawling for prawns. Only when we reached the remote outpost of Portland Roads did we find residents in a tiny little community of about seven houses, but still nowhere to get water, bread and milk. Fortunately, on Gringo we had a good reserve of water and stores, but I do believe yachts could easily run into trouble on these long lonely stretches of wilderness.

I still find it hard to conceive the vastness of this country. I think ten times the population could easily be absorbed and hardly noticed. A couple of times we shared anchorages with trawlers and usually ended up with a fresh supply of prawns. One boat wanted to swap a kilo of prawns for a razor blade. Feeling rather guilty I took over a six pack of beers as well as the razor blades. To my amazement he gave me two more kilos of king prawns and believe me the king prawns in Australia must be some of the biggest and the best in the world. The cruising life certainly suits the kids. They are both growing up strong and healthy with appetites to match - they soon made short work of devouring the prawns.

A poor sailors grave on one of the uninhabited Isles of the Barrier Reef.

We rounded Cape York, a place famous for strong currents and rough seas, in flat calm conditions and dropped anchor just behind the cape to rest for the night. The uncharacteristic conditions were so good we spent a couple of days there visiting the very friendly Wilderness Lodge and dining there. It's a place that caters for the more adventurous holiday makers, as to get there requires a drive of several days through very tough bush country with only dirt tracks to follow or, of course, a long sea journey will also get you there.

Thursday Island to me is very similar to the islands of the West Indies being populated mainly by Papua Guinean's who quite resemble the West Indians. Most of the buildings are of the old colonial type and even the climate seems the same, being buffeted by trade winds most of the time.

One of the massive dump trucks used for the bauxite mine in Gove.

After a few days there we pushed on West with a feeling of heading home having rounded the top of Australia. We crossed the Gulf of Carpentaria in style, the weather being very kind to us with full moon at night, in only two and a half days.

We entered the rather remote port of Gove from where we could check out of Australia. Gove proved to be a friendly place with a very active yacht club that made every visitor feel at home. The area is known as Arnhem Land and is owned by the Aborigines, who lease the land to a Swiss mining company for the extraction of bauxite, who in turn sell mainly to the Japanese. Everyone that works for the company seems to be on a high wage and accordingly the little town prospers nicely.

One interesting invitation we had was to visit the crocodile farm near the anchorage. Here I had the dubious pleasure of feeding a 5-meter monster with fish on the end of a stick. When he was offered the fish he promptly bit off the end of the stick as well as devouring the fish in one gulp. We all took turns to stroke one crocodile but alas he was only 12 inches long with his jaws firmly held together by his keeper. Even at that age they can still inflict a nasty bite. From the second they hatch from the egg they apparently have the instinct to snap at anything that comes near them. The keeper told us a story of a German visitor who disbelieved this and ended up with a very nasty bloody finger after having great difficultly removing the offender from the end of his finger.

Indonesia

Departing Gove on a glorious sunny morning with a gentle trade wind blowing, we felt the excitement welling inside us as we slipped out of the tranquil little bay bound for Indonesia. We wanted to pass through a narrow passage in the Wessel Islands known as "the hole in the wall" and to get the tide right was essential. To give us a good stopping off point for the trip through the narrow passage, we stopped in a group of islands with the grand name of "English Companies Islands". All uninhabited but no doubt there was once some wonderful scheme for them.

The Hole in the wall passage

Early the following morning we made our approach to the almost invisible entrance of the hole in the wall. Until you are right on top of it nothing can be seen of the opening. What an experience it was being sucked in and swept through at over 12 knots!! It's a real white-knuckle job until you are spit out into clear ocean on the other side. Apart from the exhilaration of going through the one and half mile long and about 100 yard wide passage it also acts as a short cut for any yachts heading West, saving about 35 miles of sailing. The rest of the crossing went without incident apart from being surrounded by pilot whales for half an hour. They seemed to be having a wonderful time surfing down the waves as close to the side of the boat as they could get without actually touching. It gave the children great excitement but a few palpitations for me. It was a marvellous sight.

We arrived at the town of Saumlaki in the Tanimbar Islands, a place that gets very few visiting yachts. We dropped anchor and rowed ashore to an inner harbour. We came into a scene long forgotten in most places in the world. Old engineless sailing ships with teams of men loading and unloading along gangplanks. As we rowed into the midst of it everything stopped with seemingly every eye looking at us. It was very unnerving to start with but as we pulled alongside some steps, one of them offered a hand and immediately the tension was broken. It seems they all wanted to shake our hands and showed particular interest in our blonde hair and freckles, something they had never seen among their own. We found them to be very poor but incredibly polite.

One of the many families that befriended us.

Saumlaki is a town with its own particular culture and people friendlier than anywhere we have yet been to. For the last few weeks we cruised in company with the Canadian yacht "Baron Rouge." John the skipper is always game for a laugh and at the bus stop in one little village off the beaten track he organised the locals into a dance group and had them all doing the hokey cokey while waiting for the bus!! Within minutes dozens of these happy people were coming out of their tiny houses to join in the fun. They all took turns to do their own little party pieces to humorous applause, and much laughing ensued. John and his wife, Francine, were called upon for endless encores. This all took place in the middle of the day without a drop of alcohol on anyone's lips. This was the type of spontaneous fun we had with these gentle people.

As soon as the local children came out of school they made a bee line for our boat looking for Vicky and James to go and play with them. That was the last we saw of them, for the rest of the afternoon was spent playing on their dugout canoes and sail boats.

We had an invitation into one home of a boy who had learned to speak English. His mother and father greeted us with bows and great courtesy. Inside the house was spartan and poor but very clean. Through his son acting as interpreter, the father told me we were to treat his home as our home and I would be welcome to become his son. I really believed he was very sincere in his offer but I could do nothing but stand there smiling feeling bewildered and slightly lost for words.

Before 1907 prior to the Dutch police clamping down on head hunting and cannibalism, inter-village warfare was common. In some of the out of reach areas they carried on their deadly sport until World War 2. But it seems that from vicious warriors evolved gentle and fun-loving people. Still today the interior of Yandema - the largest of the 66 islands that form the Tanimbar group - is virtually unexplored and unpopulated.

From Saumlaki we had an overnight sail to Babar where we discovered that we were only the third yacht that year to enter the port of Tepa on Babar. A couple of hours later when our friends on "Kirsten Jayne" and "Baron Rouge" arrived it was probably the first time ever that three yachts had been there all at the same time. It seemed quite an event for the locals.

We were invited to visit the local school by a teacher who spoke English and we were introduced to each class in turn. Great interest was shown in Vicky and James's blonde hair by all and the whole school wanted to make friends with them. When our tour of inspection was finished they celebrated by closing the school one and a half hours early, to the delight of all concerned. But that resulted for us in being followed by about forty children wherever we went. It wasn't so bad though as they were all well behaved and polite.

The district chief showed great interest in our venture and after an invitation to his home we returned the compliment and invited him back to the boat along with the school teacher, who had been assigned to us like a servant to act as interpreter. The chief arrived at the boat with his wife and "oos" and "ahhs" at everything they saw. Never before had the chief seen anything quite like it. He was eager to see the route we had taken and where we were going.

The village chief aboard our boat.

Always with "Oos" and "ahhh" as the interpreter explained. He then went on to say he thought we were very brave to sail all that way and he would never do anything like that. After half an hour they decided to go and have a look at the other yachts. After much bowing and handshaking they bid us 'selamat tinggal' which means 'may your actions be blessed and farewell'. Something of interest we noted in the village was the building of a new shop and house that had been built pretty well from concrete block with tiled frontage and good quality marble floors. When we asked how much a building like that would cost to erect we were told very, very expensive - 5 million rupiah. On doing a quick calculation we realised that that was only £1,500 and when we found out that the average tradesman only earns £15 per month the differential between wages and property is not that much different from England.

We departed Babar as dusk fell after the compulsory handshakes all round and the inevitable great gathering of children all waving goodbye from the beach. There can't be many places left in the world where the novelty and fascination of a visiting yacht can create such a stir, let's hope these simple happy people don't get too shaken up by progress in the future.

From Babar another overnight sail we arrived in Sermata an island as beautiful as its name, with picture postcard beaches, but the anchorage leaving a lot to be desired. In the afternoon we moved on to a much better anchorage off the northern side of Kelapa. Our two cruising companions "Baron Rouge" and "Kirsten Jayne" decided to stay the night much to their regret as neither got a wink of sleep due to the incoming swell. The snatching on the anchor chain was so bad that "Kirsten Jayne" snapped their nylon strop that's used to cushion the sudden pull of a chain in swell.

The following night was spent in a rather precarious spot anchored on the edge of a reef off the island of Moa. As we were feeling tired and the weather settled we decided to make do. However, our anchor was in fifteen meters of water and when the boat dropped back over the ridge it was so deep that no sounding could be recorded, even though our echo sounder was set on the 200 meter range.

Moa is an island that very rarely gets visitors, simply because there is no anchorage there or airstrip. Its small population is very primitive and isolated, untouched by the outside world. We didn't get the much needed sleep we needed that night because it was difficult to relax in such a spot with the chain rumbling on the coral very few minutes. Also in the still of the air natives were having some sort of ritual on the beach with singing and chanting and what appeared to be the slaughtering of an unlucky pig. The squealing went on for some time and coming from the darkness, with only the light from a fire and a couple of fire torches it conveyed a very eerie atmosphere hardly inductive to sleep. We thought it prudent not to go ashore.

At first light, we upped anchor and pointed West again, intending to sail south of Wetar. The wind increased in strength gradually forcing us to go north about between the islands of Kisar and Romang. On this tack the sailing was excellent with the boat holding a solid 7.5 knots all day. Alas in the evening the wind eventually died forcing us to motor for most of the night. In the shelter of Wetars 4,000 feet high mountains I doubt whether it would ever be possible to sail this coast anyway.

Still pushing West for the island of Alor, as dawn broke a breeze sprang up from the South giving us a close haul to our destination. After only a few hours though it died away to a total calm.

Our second night at sea saw us motoring along the North coast of this strange island - Alor. It is so rugged that travel is almost impossible inland so its people are isolated from each other, split into some 50 different tribes with almost as many languages. The interior is still so little effected by the outside world that apparently only 30 years ago heads were still being hunted. Its villages are built on the tops of hills like fortresses with steep sides so that horses were useless and trails on foot impossible during the rainy season.

On Alor one of the strangest customs is the use of Mokos, an hourglass shaped bronze drum with sheet bronze instead of skin on its ends. There are thousands of them apparently found buried in the ground believed to be gifts from the Gods. They are, by later historians, thought to have come from the old Doggone culture of China. Maybe the people of Alor buried them as a gift to their spirits in now forgotten times. Today the Mokos have acquired enormous value among the Alorese whose men try to amass them in order to buy a bride. Today the Mokos are also sought after by outsiders who are willing to pay far more than the poor natives could ever afford. The Government has passed a law now to stop Mokos from leaving the island.

We met one of the local school teachers who spoke reasonable English. After a little bartering he agreed to act as our guide and very good he was too. One of the things we wanted to do was to get totally off the beaten track and into the interior to see some of the remote and primitive villages. Luck was on our side as he said he knew of just such a place. So, after a bit more bartering, we hired one of the local minibuses. Off we set the next morning along some very crude roads in the direction of a village named Wolwal along with our guide Mohammed. After a couple of hours of travel, with a motion similar to being in a hot cement mixer, we arrived at our destination. The reception we had was astonishing. At first the children ran and hid from us, the braver ones keeping at a safe distance with puzzled looks on their faces. After a little coaxing by Mohammed and Sadie blowing up some balloons they gradually crept forward one by one with trepidation. On speaking to Mohammed we found out that the children had never seen a white man. The chief of the village came to meet us and invited us to his hut. He offered us coconuts to drink that were more than welcome after our journey. I asked about the ancient Mokos and after a debate amongst themselves they very carefully brought out six and proudly placed them before us for inspection. By this time the locals had become a little more familiar with us and swarmed in a great mass all around the hut.

The village chief shows James how to use a bow and arrow

It was a little claustrophobic but at no time did we feel the slightest bit threatened, even though there were hunters around with very powerful bows and arrows. Having gone there with a good supply of cigarettes and sweets we soon became very popular and were treated like royalty. Wherever we went through the village bamboo chairs appeared, as if by magic, to sit down every time we stopped for a minute. Always with an entourage of people swarming around us.

As usual one of the great fascinations to them was our children's blonde hair. Hands would slip through the crowd to touch and quickly disappear again into the mass of people. James showed interest in the bows and arrows of the hunters and one gave a display of marksmanship. From thirty paces, he put an arrow straight through the trunk of a banana tree. After which we were presented with a beautifully made hunting bow and two arrows by the chief.

Upon leaving the whole population of the village of Wolwal turned out to see us off. Old ladies, hunters, chiefs and crowds of children all stood waving us goodbye as the minibus edged its way through the people and slowly out of the village. Until only a few years ago these people were considered savages by the missionaries, but we found them to be very human, kind and generous people.

If you need a canoe each, cut one in half.

Whilst in Alor James had been playing most days with the local children on their canoes. We thought it might be an idea to get him one of his own so I enquired where we might buy one and was immediately shown one or two that were for sale. After the compulsory bargaining we came away with a very nice dugout canoe, about three meters long made from a single piece of wood and not too heavy to carry on deck. We bought it for pricey sum of 35,000 rupees. It might sound a lot, but converted to sterling that totals about £9. It will save a lot of wear and tear on our over-worked dinghy, now that James has his own transport. After practicing for a few hours he perfected the art of rolling over, emptying the water out and climbing back in while in deep water, which is a lot more difficult than it sounds. It requires a nimble bit of balancing with the palms of the hands flat on the bottom of the canoe and a quick flick of the leg to get a foot over the side, followed by a little bit of contortionism to get the backside in. No matter how I tried I could not perfect the skill and I doubt I ever will but then kids do learn a lot quicker than adults.

From Alor we cruised on along the chain of Indonesian Islands. We past Pantar and Lomblens huge mountains on our port side and the Comba volcano to starboard, with a gentle trail of white smoke drifting from its peak. The following morning as the sun rose in the East and the full moon sank in the West, we had our next anchorage on the horizon - Pula Besar on the Island of Flores. This was the third island during our circumnavigation that we visited with the same name.

One of the things yachtsmen have to come to terms with is the constant boarding by locals throughout Indonesia. Wherever you drop anchor within a few minutes canoes are alongside and invariably three or four locals climb aboard without invitation. They will remain on board, just sitting on the cabin roof for half an hour or so, after the formal "Selamat Pagi" (good morning). This I believe is an extension of their village lives where boundaries do not exist. One item that really fascinated them was the pegs we used for hanging out the washing. They had never seen any before. People, and sometimes hordes of children, seemed to stroll in and out or through anyone's hut without question and without any challenge from the apparent owners. Sometimes when boarded one will come forward and ask to see passports and cruising permits before leaving in their canoes. Some of the more forward ones are interested in learning English or teaching us Indonesian. Many an hour was spent on the aft deck trying to make conversation with our limited Indonesian and their broken English. One of the things they learned quickly was to ask for cigarettes. This only applied to the more westerly islands of the chain, further east yachts are very infrequent visitors and are still treated with a little trepidation and curiosity.

Sadie had a routine of learning two or three useful words a day and within a few weeks it was amazing how well she got through a conversation. Although not too good myself, I believe Indonesian is quite an easy language to learn and often one word covers a lot of meanings. For example, the word 'berapa' can be how much a thing costs or how many or how heavy.

We always landed up with children around us. They were always polite and well behaved.

We have been pushing on west now for the last couple of weeks in an effort to get to Bali by the end of September. By November there is a possibility of the North-West winds setting in, which would make our trip up to Singapore very difficult indeed. For the last three weeks now we haven't seen any yacht or person from Western society. Tomorrow on the western end of Flores we may meet up with other cruising yachts heading our way who have come up from Darwin. It's always nice to meet up with other yachties to swap a few anecdotes, perhaps over a beer, in some strange and distant port. After a night and day we arrived at Bajo but to our surprise still no yachts, although we did see two or three white people ashore.

Sailing along this coast at night can be perilous as quite large Indonesian craft ply these waters under sail with no navigation lights other than the glow of a cigarette from the helmsman. On a few occasions we had to divert our course after picking up the tell-tale bleep on the radar and indeed, on one occasion, I'm sure a head-on collision was avoided thanks to the radar. Only when the oncoming sailboat went drifting by, about 20 meters abeam of us, was the silhouette faintly visible. Most of these boats are built of massively strong proportions - I think you would have little chance of surviving a head-on collision with one. The other factor that stops you from nodding off during a night watch is that no sort of rescue service exists within a thousand miles

Bajo was a real shanty town with little market stalls all over the place. They seemed to be open from early morning until ten at night. During an evening stroll through the village it was a pretty sight with each stall having a solitary light bulb hanging down with a few nocturnal moths fluttering around in the still, hot night air. The stall holders sit at their stalls ever patient in the hope of one last customer and are always ready with a grin from ear to ear. Even though Indonesia seems to be engulfed in poverty, as in other poor countries we have visited, the people appear to be just as happy as those in the more affluent countries. Maybe it is a case of never missing what you have never had.

Komodo Dragons

The following day we did a short 15 mile hop to Rinja Island. On the ancient charts it's proclaimed "thar be dragons" and that's what we were hoping to see. We hired a guide at 7 a.m and off we tramped. Even early in the morning the heat was oppressive but we were well rewarded for our efforts with fabulous views of groups of monkeys feeding in the early morning sunlight. Also, great herds of deer roamed free giving the occasional yap very similar to the sound of a dog. Our guide was getting a little frustrated after about 2 hours at not being able to find one of the elusive Komodo dragons. The tell-tale signs were all around us with the skulls and vertebrae of long since deceased buffalo that had fallen victims to the dragons. In the dense forest we disturbed wild boar and horses until eventually our guide picked up the trail of a dragon. Then after a lot of quiet trekking through dense thicket we came across our elusive friend.

Rinja on the horizon

It was about 8ft long with a huge forked tongue smelling the air. He was well aware of our presence and kept one eye on us as we moved. We managed to get about 15ft from him but our guard was concerned for our safety and advised against getting closer, because these creatures are quite capable of bringing down wild buffalo and devouring the whole thing in about three days.

We left Rinja for Komodo trying to figure out the direction of the current between the two islands that can run up to 7 knots on springs. In Komodo we saw a rather gruesome display of a goat being slaughtered and thrown into a pit full of overweight Komodo dragons. It was all laid on for the boat loads of visitors that arrive here every day. It was not as interesting as tracking one down in its natural environment. We did at least though get a very close-up look at the pre-historic reptiles tearing their unfortunate breakfast to pieces.

Komodo Dragones in abundance devouring an unfortunate goat

From here we pushed on hard covering sixty-five miles in daylight hours, with an average of one knot adverse current to reach Sumbawa. The temperature at 8 a.m. was 28 degrees celsius and by mid-day was 34 degrees, so on reaching our sheltered anchorage at Bima a long laze in the cool sea was a real treat. We met up with an American Yatch named "Out of Here" from California, the first yacht for nearly a month. On sailing along the coast they had landed a huge wahoo and very kindly invited us over for a very pleasant evening meal. By 8.30 p.m we found it difficult to keep our eyes open. James fell asleep on the side deck and by 9.30p.m including

107

our hosts, we were all asleep in bed. The following day saw us sailing along the foothills of the giant Tambora volcano that blew its top in 1850 at the expense of 8,000 lives. It now stands at almost 10,000ft and apparently takes three days of hard slog to ascend to its peak. The climber is to be rewarded with multi coloured lakes at the top. In the intense heat I can't imagine how anyone could ever make it up there. Every day we have been in Indonesia the temperature has been around the 32-34 degrees celsius mark. The slightest exertion sees one soaking wet perspiration. Fortunately the hot air makes the sea seem nice and cool which makes for a real treat to have a soak in after a long day's sail.

Bali. Land of Temples

Bali was eventually reached on the 27th October after 2,000 miles of sailing from our first Indonesian landfall of Tanimbar. Everywhere you look in Bali you can't help seeing the heads of Gods carved over doorways, on the corner of buildings, or incorporated in the garden wall. The Balinese have their own form of Hinduism. Every morning offerings are put out to the spirits who are believed to be everywhere. The offerings are believed to pay homage to the good spirits and to placate the bad ones. You just can't get away from religion in Bali, with three incredible ornate temples in each village no matter how small the village. Every field has a shrine in the corner and almost every home has a shrine in the front garden. The good thing is their religion is a happy religion and not fatalistic; even their funerals are a happy occasion with singing, dancing and generally having a good time to celebrate the release of the spirit.

The strange and fascinating Island of Bali

From the building of temples a tremendous talent of carvers has evolved using wood, stone or anything else they can lay their hands on. Throughout Bali some very lovely carvings can be purchased, usually in ebony and very finely carved.

Primitive methods of ploughing as still used throughout the far east.

We hired a car for five days to visit the mountainous interior, staying at unique hotels set into the side of cliffs, on the side of lakes and planted onto the side of mountains. One such place was the palace of the Royal family of Bali. All rooms can be bartered for and once away from the tourist traps they work out incredibly cheap. Even the palace at Ubud was less than $40 for the four of us. James spent the best part of the day playing with the Royal family's children who were in residence at the time. Our room there was incredibly ornately carved and most was original from the 16th century. Sadly, amidst the splendour of palaces and temples, poverty abounds in Bali with the majority of people struggling to survive. In the countryside the picturesque labour-intensive paddy fields strive to produce enough rice to keep its expanding population fed, even though most fields produce three crops a year.

The children helping to thresh the rice

All the rice is planted, reaped and threshed by hand. Everyone from young children to old grandmas work in the paddy fields along with oxen to pull the old wooden ploughs through the heavy soil between crops. We stopped the ·car and went for a walk along the walls of the paddy fields to meet a group of workers with the men reaping with scythes and the women threshing the ripe crop. Immediately we were greeted with friendly smiles and waves. Within minutes James and Vicky were trying their hand at threshing the rice from its stems- simply by hitting a handful of stems against the sides of sloping boards, so the rice falls to the ground.

Singapore and The Malacca Straits

The time was pushing us on again to make a move north before the north-west monsoons set in, so provisioning started once again in earnest to prepare for the thousand-mile sail to Singapore. We sailed out of Benoa harbour feeling more than a little sad to be leaving the beautiful land of Bali with its strange cultures but did have Singapore and Malaysia to look forward to.

Our initial plan was to do short hops of maybe two-day legs but with fair winds and flat seas we set off and just kept going for six days and nights until the island of Serutu was reached. We found a snug anchorage on the North coast where a fresh water stream entered the sea, with cool clear water down from the mountains. We had a welcome rest there for a couple of days before heading off across the South China Sea for Linga, an island about 100 miles south of Singapore. This is a stretch of water notorious for piracy. Suffering with no wind and a hot, humid climate we felt it prudent to push on and not hang around. We motored on non-stop for three days until Lingo was reached, where the usual friendly welcome of dugout canoes came out to meet us. Throughout this area many houses are built on stilts above the water. At night time a net is lowered underneath and raised periodically, thus providing the family with a fresh supply of fish every day.

From here we day-hopped via Bitang to Singapore. The channel running across the southern end of Singapore is the world's busiest shipping lane with ships nose to tail streaming East or West in their set lanes. Off the South coast of Singapore there are never less than fifty ships at anchor. It makes for a yachtsman's nightmare with a ship entering or leaving Singapore harbour every two minutes. It's a bit like crossing a busy high street with leviathan ships instead of cars and buses. One can only wonder in amazement at what they all bring in and take out.

Singapore doesn't seem to produce too many things and appears to be one huge trading depot. Somehow it works and financially it seems a great success. The pressure of life there was too much for us though and after 10 days there we felt worn out.

Singapore has thrown off its old image of street traders and corner shops and moved into the 20th century with a bang. Everything is ultra modern from its high rise building to its railway or M.R.T as it is called, which stands for Mass Rapid Transport. In the city without a Mercedes or cell phone you don't count as anyone. Status in

Singapore is everything to the businessman. Some of the exclusive clubs cost as much as $80,000 to join and even their membership is oversubscribed. Though we were a little disenchanted with Singapore and thought a number of its people robot like, we did have a few pleasant experiences there.

(far right) Dr Peter Ng and his family who took good care of us in Singapore.

On visiting the doctor to restock on Malaria tablets and antibiotics he wanted to know what we needed them for. When we explained he immediately showed great enthusiasm and invited us to his home for a meal. That night he picked us up in his Mercedes and chaperoned us to his scrupulously clean house. His wife and parents greeted us with lots of bowing and hand shaking, in true Chinese style, after removing our shoes before entry. They went on to be the model of perfect hosts with an incredible variety of true Chinese food laid on for us and lively conversation.

Doctor Peter Ng and his wife Edna were enthused about the places we had visited and people we had met. They said they had always dreamed of doing something similar. They made us promise to drop them cards from time to time before chauffeuring us back to our boat. They said we could stay with them anytime we ever go to

Singapore again. Whether we go back again is doubtful, but who knows.

On 3rd of November we pulled out of Changi harbour and wove our way through the maze of ships bound for the notorious Malacca Straits. As we left Singapore in the still, early morning light a blanket of fumes and exhaust gases could be seen sitting over its already bustling city as it awoke to a new day. We managed to get the tide right and received an extra push of two knots for the first six hours. Reaching Raffles light house and turning north for our approach to the Malacca Straits the tide turned with us to push us north, giving us an average of 7.3 knots for 57 miles.

An incredible array of foods on offer at the local market in Singapore.

Along the Malacca Straits we sailed during the day and anchored at night for the 250 miles to Port Kelang, only stopping off to visit the ancient trading town of Malacca. Most of the city dates back to the 16th century. It was once a major link with the East and the West, trading in silks, spices and gold. First ruled by the Portuguese then by the Dutch and then in 1824 by the British until 1957.

Unfortunately in the mid 19th Century the river silted up and caused decline in the prosperity of the town. All the old town still remains much as it did then and simply oozes with the atmosphere of a bygone age. The old Chinese traders still ply their wares from the ancient shops, probably much the same today as 200-300 years ago. A walk into any shop in the old town gives one a culture and history lesson all in one. Dealing with any shopkeeper is a real pleasure, they are polite and trustworthy, as only the old Chinese shopkeepers can be. Malaysia is a very forward thinking country moving quickly to becoming a powerful economic power. Fortunately they are also proud of their history and striving to maintain Malacca and its ancient waterfront exactly as it has always been.

The ancient trading town of Malacca.

We had to anchor the boat about a mile offshore and came in by dinghy so we couldn't spend as much time there as we would have liked. It was just as well that we did get back to the boat when we did as the wind piped up later in the afternoon, which would have been a very tricky trip back indeed in a dinghy. Later on that night we anchored behind a little island. We caught the full brunt of an incredible storm, with lightening bouncing off the sea all around us and rain like it can only rain in the tropics. It came down so heavily it was difficult to breathe when I went on the foredeck to let out more chain because of 35 knot gusts of wind. Fortunately for us the tiny island and reef broke the quickly rising seas before they got to us.

We didn't get much sleep though as the anchorage still became very rolly. We couldn't risk putting to sea because of the numerous fishing nets in the area often stretching half a mile or more across our path.

To run into one of these on a dark windy night is my worst nightmare. So we had no option but to stay put and ride the storm out at anchor. Having a choice though I would have preferred to be in open water as there is far less strain on a boat when it can ride waves freely rather than snubbing the anchor chain. As soon as daylight broke we upped anchor and pushed on towards Port Kelang. By this time though the wind and seas had moderated with no sign of last night's turmoil. I realised last night's fireworks display was on the 5th November – very apt I thought, but we would have preferred a good night's sleep instead.

The following night we had a disturbance of a different kind. Being anchored in a bay just north of Port Dixon all was well and we settled in for a good night's rest. About 11 p.m. the kids came running into our cabin to say that someone was on deck. I leapt out of bed and up the companionway just in time to see a man making his way to the aft deck to where the outboard engine for the dinghy was clamped on. Upon my appearance, he quickly made a retreat and said he was just checking over the boat. I warned him he was playing a very dangerous game as all boats in this area are on guard for piracy and carry guns. "You stand a very good chance of getting yourself shot". At which point he retreated and apologised for disturbing us. He climbed into the waiting dinghy and drifted away. It was fortunate for us the children saw the torch light shine through a port hole and raised the alarm. Piracy is on everyone's mind around the Malacca Strait area. I do believe these two men were just simple fishermen trying for a new outboard for their dinghy. So far this was the closest we had come to having anything disappear. In fact most people in these parts who have anything at all seem intent on giving you something or other.

The Raja Muda

From Port Kelang we joined the Raja Muda race to Langkawi which is split into three overnight legs. The yacht race is sponsored by the King of Malaysia and Heineken Lager. The night before the race we all gathered at the Royal Selangor Yacht Club for a meal and to be introduced to his Highness the Crown Prince. All the participants lined up, including crews.

The Crown Prince joins us for breakfast.

We stood very formally with the children each side of us. His Royal Highness was very friendly and polite but when he leaned forward to shake our six-year-old son's hand, James said "Guess what?" "Pardon," said the Crown Prince "Guess what?" James repeated, by this time we were all cringing, "What?" replied the Prince. "You're the second King I've met" said James, having previously met the King of Tonga. It struck the Prince and everyone around as being funny and everyone descended into fits of laughter. The future King was obviously not offended as the next morning, while having breakfast before the race, he came over to our table and asked if he could join us. He asked us all about our circumnavigation, being a keen sailor himself he was eager to learn the problems likely to be encountered. He took part in two legs of the race in his own boat and was a very competitive sailor.

The following day when the race started, the wind was so light over the first two legs that very few cruising yachts finished. All but a very determined handful ended up motoring including ourselves.

From the word go at the Royal Selanger Yacht Club in Port Kalang it turned out to be one big party with eating and drinking, like one does on Christmas Day for a whole week and endless supplies of food and drink. It was a real test of one's stamina just to keep pace with the partying let alone the racing. One of our favourite ports of call at the end of the second leg was Penang. Once the home of countless wealthy British in the days of colonialism, all that remains today are the numerous huge houses. A few are beautifully maintained but sadly many have fallen into decay. The legacy of the once proud owners, they look forlorn standing in their overgrown gardens that were no doubt once manicured and nurtured. No matter how many of these houses we looked at. They all seemed to have the same air of sadness about them.

Just a memory of a bygone era. Progress marches on however and the new forward-thinking people of Penang are rapidly catching up, if not overtaking Western society. The bridge built between Malaya and Penang is the third longest bridge in the world. We had breakfast in a restaurant fifty-nine stories up, overlooking the new city rising up and up out of the old. One place that has retained its old-world charm though is the Eastern and Oriental Hotel. Once a favourite retreat of the rich and famous, it still echoes the ambience of that period of time when Ernest Hemingway and Somerset Maugham once strolled its palatial rooms. On the third leg we spent a blustery night bashing into 25 knots of wind up to Langkawi. Again in the evening the prize giving was one great feast of food, booze and dancing. At breakfast time there was a distinct quietness as everyone nursed their sore heads. That morning we had the honour of having the Crown Prince, Raja Muda, join us for breakfast again. After the end of the race party most of the participants had drifted away when the MC got on the microphone and said, "We have a problem here

There are about two thousands tins of Heineken Beer left and we don't know what to do with them. Does anyone want them?". That night, along with our friend Tom, we went back to our boats with little freeboard left on our dinghies. It lasted us for months.

One of the many decorative roofs on the old buildings of Penang

Whilst in Langkawi we had heard talk of an inland lake at the centre of an island about 10 miles south. The next day off we set in pursuit of this lake and possibly a little adventure to the island of Pulau Dayung Bunting. Langkawi is part of a group of 103 islands and a trip weaving one's way through the totally unspoilt archipelago is a yachtman's delight. Arriving at the aforesaid island we boarded the dinghy to the shore and found the start of the path through the dense bush. The freshwater lake that now replaces the fire of a volcano crater had the desired cooling effect on entering its clear water. We spent most of the afternoon bathing and picnicking in the tranquil, verdant environment of dense Malayan jungle, feeling very content with ourselves on finding such a wonderful place.

We used Langkawi as a place to stock up, it being a duty-free port. Later on we were to regret not buying more as in Thailand the prices more than doubled on drink and food.

We anchored off many strange Islands like this in Thailand

A gentle breeze and flat sea prevailed for the rest of the trip up to Thailand. Thailand must be one the greatest cruising grounds in the world as far as scenery goes. Ao Phangnga Bay on the East coast of Phuket is truly spectacular. Islands rise up out of the sea to over a thousand feet with spectacular overhangs that make them look as if they are about to fall over. Several of the islands have tunnels through which the dinghy could be taken at low tide and into lagoons at the centre of the island. One such tunnel at Ko Phanak is over 200 yards long. We made our way through with our friends Tom and Sherida from the yacht "Distant Song" and with the aid of a tilley lamp and torch, we emerged out in the centre of the island to the most amazing lake with sheer cliffs all around undercut at the base with giant stalactite's hanging down just above the water.

Any sound echoed around the quietness of the huge crater. The only noise to be heard was the occasional squeak of a bat. We couldn't stay too long because when the tide rises the entrance of the cave becomes too low to get the dinghy through. As beautiful as the area was we didn't fancy spending about nine hours sitting in the dinghy.

A whole village built on stilts

From Ko Phanak we pushed further North to visit the island where the James Bond Film "The man with the Golden Gun" was made. An island amid dozens of other incredibly spectacular islands all rising up out of the sea in breath taking rock formations of a million individual sculptures, not of modern art, for these carvings have been around since time began. The only chisels used are wind and water. We anchored for the night off the island of Koh Yang and went ashore to visit the solitary family that live here to arrange a trip we had heard about up to a Muslim village.

The next morning off we roared in their ancient carved out long tail boat, as they are so aptly named, weaving our way through the channels, tunnels and mangrove rivers with the tell-tale plume of water shooting up from behind our boat from where the name derives. After just over an hour we arrived at our destination much the richer for our experience. The village was built on stilts, in the shallows of the Khlong Phangnga River was, stranger than fiction, in so much as we never did find out the name of the place. If indeed there was a name I couldn't find it on any of the charts or guides. Apparently the Thai government refused to give the place recognition or to accept any of the inhabitants as Thai people. Presumably it is because they never buy any land as whenever an extension is needed they simply drive a few more piles into the estuary bed and expand their living area. Hence the village has grown into a small town and prospers nicely in spite of the fact that it has no access by road. It has become quite a tourist attraction with restaurants and side-walks in a tiny world of its own.

We celebrated Christmas in true style aboard the yacht "Distant Song" with a real Christmas dinner of roast turkey with all the trimmings.

After cruising these waters for a week we got back to civilisation at Krabi, on the mainland, and duly indulged in the dozens of low priced restaurants there.

From Krabi we sailed, after Christmas, back to Phuket to pick up the rest of our mail. New Year was duly celebrated at Patong Bay along with 87 other yachts to the greatest display of fireworks one could ever imagine. The eastern people have always been keen on firework displays and this lived up to expectation in spectacular proportions. How the town avoided being burned down we'll never know as the whole area was showered in sparks continuously from 8.00am to 12.30am.

A couple of days later we heard the rather frightening news that an earthquake had struck the island of Flores, sending a tidal wave as high as tops of trees across the island, killing nearly 2,000 people. When we considered it had only been two months since we were there, it put us in a very sober mood

On checking out of Thailand our trip very nearly came to an end. I was approached by a man who claimed to be interested in purchasing a boat the same as ours. One thing led to another and before the day was through, he ended up making a very respectable offer for Gringo. With a depressed market in England we thought it might make a lot of economic sense to accept such an offer while the going was good. So we agreed to sell with rather a heavy heart. The toughest part came the next day as we sat and watched our cruising companions depart for Sri Lanka. The week that followed we felt terribly alone as by now most of the other cruising yachts heading West had left.

After keeping us on tenterhooks for ten days our prospective buyer announced that he couldn't raise the money for four months. Had the deal fallen through in that time we would have been stranded in Thailand for a whole year. Once the trade winds of the Northeast monsoon are missed it becomes almost impossible to sail west to the Red Sea. Not only are the winds against you but there is a high risk of typhoons.

A decision was reached in about three-seconds flat and the following evening we were on our way to Sri Lanka - 1,100 miles away. Inside we were secretly glad.

The Indian Ocean

What a sail we had!! In 48 hours we had reached the Nicobar Islands, over 300 miles away. On the third day out we equalled our best run ever with a little over 172 miles in 24 hours. It was as though Gringo was straining to catch up with our friends and to escape the clutches of Thailand. Anyway, she was certainly free now pressing on at sometimes 8 knots with a huge bone in her teeth from the bow wave.

We were already well into the Indian Ocean on our way across the Bay of Bengal after only three days. Gradually we have settled into the old, now familiar routine of life at sea but sometimes odd things occur on a crossing. Last night during Sadie's watch she was bombarded by a shoal of flying fish that for some reason seemed to make a bee line for her. Several bouncing off her in the pitch dark gave her a rude awakening. When I went to investigate what was happening she was surrounded by smelly little fish.

Checking noon day sighting to make sure our Sat Nav was still behaving

On the **Tuesday and Wednesday 19th/20th January** we again topped our best 24 hour run with 182 miles noon to noon. Over the past week our 24 hours runs read 140, 160, 172, 182, 172, 156. We pushed on as never before through boisterous seas, seas as old as time itself but with new patterns every second that last but a second and then are gone forever. It felt good to be at sea again away from the masses but life is a compromise as we were also looking forward to seeing our cruising friends again, with whom we had developed a close affinity over the many miles together.

On **Thursday the 21st January** we were hoping we might sight land. In the meantime, at long last, we managed to land a 15lb tuna, but not before losing one lure and then losing a fish after a fifteen-minute struggle. Just as we got him alongside he made one last dive and managed to free himself off the hook. This second one however wasn't so lucky. Sadie rounded up the boat and with sails flogging our prey was landed on deck. Having run out of fresh meat two days ago it was like a present from above.

We arrived in Sri Lanka in only 6 1/2 days of sailing 1,100 miles, in record time for us. Sri Lanka seems to be a mixture of cultures with Buddhism being the main religion, followed by Hinduism and Christianity. It was first ruled by the Portuguese, then the Dutch and finally the British until 1946. Along with a change of name from Ceylon to Sri Lanka it acquired a democratic government from that date on. Unfortunately, as in most third world countries, bureaucracy seems to hold everything up and nothing happens without someone's palm being greased. That includes the checking in procedure for yachts that costs an astronomical US $130. Even the Port Captain boards your boat asking for gifts. However, having worked your way through the bureaucracy and paid your money the interior is very beautiful with bush jungle right up to the edge of the towns.

Many of the towns are bustling places with hundreds of makeshift stalls of wood and corrugated iron sheet. Most of them leave a lot to be desired in the way of hygiene. Walking through one of these villages a Mahout (an elephant owner/trainer) was coming in the opposite direction with the biggest elephant we had ever seen. We stood in awe, looking at the giant beast, when the man offered a ride on him. We all offered the ride to Sadie who was none too pleased but after a bit of encouragement decided to give it a go. The elephant was impeccably behaved and lifted his front leg for Sadie to use as a step to climb aboard. By this time there was a lot of encouragement from the gathering crowd of on-lookers. With the help of the elephant himself and numerous hands pushing and shoving she ended up lying face down over the animals back. With further struggling and gripping she eventually managed to get her leg over, only to realise its head was behind her!! Somehow, she managed to get on facing backwards. By this time there must have been fifty villagers around us all crying with laughter. The only one not amused was Sadie.

Sadie eventually climbed on the elephant, but the wrong way

In Galle we met up with our old friend Sven who was on the last leg of his second solo circumnavigation in a 5.5 meter yacht. Not bad going for a 60-year-old man. He's just about finishing his third book too. He did hint to us however that he may give up sailing his tiny boat when he gets back to Denmark. He says he would like a little comfort in his old age. What a life this truly remarkable sailor has had, fulfilling ambitions that most men can only dream about in his quiet professional way and with a true love of people of all ages, races and creeds. The sailing that he has undertaken makes our circumnavigation seem a piece of cake.

We enjoyed our stay in Sri Lanka, visiting the world's largest Buddha, seeing the working elephants and other tourist attractions. As you probably gather we prefer if possible, to get off the beaten track. One such visit took us to a tea factory in the lowlands.

It was like a step back in time with huge old Ruston diesel engines producing power to drive machinery and furnaces burning old rubber trees to dry the tea leaves. It was once the pride and joy of a wealthy colonist but now unfortunately, as with most old houses in this part of the world, the ageing mansion has fallen prey to the ravages of time and is now home only to a colony of bats that flutter around the rooms as we encroach on their private domain and former splendour. The factory is now owned by a Sri Lankan who keeps the factory producing 24 hours a day, 7 days a week with three shift workers that earn $1 a day for their toil.

Galle lighthouse   *The worlds largest Budha.*

On **Wednesday 27th January** we pulled gently out of Galle harbour bidding our few remaining friends farewell, bound for the open ocean and Oman, 1700 miles away. We clawed our way to gain ground from the coast in an effort to pick up the North-East trade winds, pushing into 15 knots of wind. The sea was out of proportion for the wind strength. The bow spirit often poked its end into the steep confused seas, stopping the boat dead in her tracks.
In the middle of the night we finally broke free of our bonds and found the trades that funnel between India and Sri Lanka. Very

gentle at first but at least enough to fill our sails and reduce the uncomfortable motion. It later slowly increased to 25 knots on the beam, still with very confused seas and occasionally breakers, smashing into the side of the boat.

We pressed on at good speed through the pitch black night. The sun coming up in the East was a welcome sight after the long night, first a dim red glow that gradually broke out into its full glory, chasing away the clouds, reflecting pure white on the breaking wave caps around us. Suddenly all seemed well as we charged along in cascades of froth bursting from the bows. The following two days were the sort of sailing you normally only read about in fiction books with perfect winds and clear blue skies in the day, followed by nights amass with a million bright stars. In the North, we could see Polaris and the Plough. To the South we could see the Southern Cross. Alas nothing lasts forever and midday on the 29th February the wind started to fail. We struggled on under every stitch of canvas we could carry until we ground to a virtual standstill. We had to resort to burning the diesel to keep us moving. In the afternoon we had a visit from a school of whales but little else to do other than read books.

According to the weather printouts they showed north easterly winds right the way across the Indian Ocean to Aden in Yemen, but for some reason we were getting very light southerlies. Being over 100 miles from the coast of India I would not have thought it was the effect of the land. We had no choice but to motor on otherwise it meant wallowing at the pace of a snail. The next couple of days we still pursued our goal in the light winds. We reached the stage where we couldn't afford more diesel as a real risk of running out was becoming imminent if we continued to run the engine as we had over the last few days. We were not even a third of the way across. To makes matters worse we encountered a 1.5 knot current.

Monday 1st February. The breeze has now picked up from the North East giving us a gentle sail in the right direction. In the morning we hooked into a good size fish that played around with me for about 15 minutes before making an incrediblyhigh-speed run. The clutch on the reel started to smoke just before the inevitable happened. Twang went the line loosing my good lure and trace. The fish never even broke the surface of the water.

We often resorted to making our own fishing lures, using the finger of a rubber glove. I would draw two eyes with an indelible pen and shred the base to make it look vaguely like a squid. I then tied a hook through the centre. It often proved effective and we caught many fish with this type of lure.

A good size bonito caught with one of my home made lures.

Tuesday 2nd February. The sun rose to a gloriously good day with about 12 knots of breeze on the beam and clear blue skies. Our spirits are high today as we bound along towards Oman. We have been picking up the BBC World Service over the last few days with regard to fighting in the Middle East. We are still not sure of the reception we will get from the Arab's when we reach port. In the afternoon I spoke to a ship heading in the opposite direction called "World Brasilia". The skipper said there should be no problem for us up the Red Sea, but the American's are searching ships heading south to see if they are shipping arms. The skipper asked if there was anything we needed before heading on to Singapore. It made us feel good to sense camaraderie between people of all nations at sea.

Sailing in home waters we very rarely make contact with ships, but out in the oceans it seems quite a natural thing to do. Probably because during long watches on the bridge of ships they get a little bored and to have a chat with a passing yacht breaks the monotony for them.

In the past I have found most ships very helpful in confirming positions for us or giving weather forecasts. Once when my old Walker Sat Nav decided to stop working I had to resort to using my Sextant and sight reduction tables working out position with sun run sun and dead reckoning method. I would take a sun sight two hours before noon, one at midday and then another sighting two hours after high noon to give me my position and then keep a careful eye on the heading and distance covered.

The first time I ever had to resort to the old method of navigating I was amazed just how accurate it is. After five days I spotted a ship and gave them a call, to find out I was just half a mile away from where I thought I was which is nothing in a big ocean.

Being keen to close the gap between our present position and Oman I decided to take the 9 degree channel north of the Maldives and South of the Lakshadweep Isles. At one point a decision was made to call at Suheli Par, the southernmost Lakshadweep Isle but timing was well out as we passed by at 2 a.m. The wind had filled from the North East giving us a good sail so we saw no reason to interrupt our routine by hoving too for the night, to wait for daylight, so on we pressed.

Wednesday 3rd February. Started off to be a good day. At 2a.m we landed the best fish for a long time - a 20lb Dorado. We haven't caught one of those since the Pacific. They are probably one of the best fish there is to eat. The flesh is nice and white when it comes straight from the sea into the frying pan and it just melts in your mouth.

Throughout the day we had good sailing but the night time was a different story. We had wind alright, but not quite enough and an awkward swell came from the North causing the boat to roll from gunnel to gunnel all night. On every roll the sails would empty and then fill with a tremendous bang. The incessant noise grated on our nerves. As the sails emptied you would sit with your teeth clenched waiting for the crash as the boat started on the reciprocal roll. In spite of running off course, 25 degrees, I just could not get rid of the uncomfortable motion. It was one of those occasions when it seemed impossible to get the boat to sail where you want it to go. I'm sure if there had been another three knots of wind it would have been no problem. It would have been enough just to keep the sails full.

The morning of the 4th arrived and even though feeling very tired we couldn't help but feel better as the day bloomed into a glorious cloudless day.

Schooling and breakfast often combined at sea.

Friday 5th February. We managed to sail all night in spite of our poor old spinnaker eventually giving up on us. For no apparent reason it decided to tear in half in about 7 knots of wind. So in the morning the sewing machine came out. It turned out to be an industrious day for us with about 4 hours sewing to repair the sail. I don't know how long it will last as the sun has made the material brittle. Then I had a trip up the main mast to repair the sender for the wind instruments that somehow got bent out of alignment. Whilst up there I managed to check the spinnaker halyard blocks and mast head Stroud fittings and all seemed to be in good order. To round the day off nicely we landed a Dorado fish just before dusk, only a small one but just enough for tomorrow's dinner for the four of us. On top of all this the sailing was superb all day with a steady 12 knots on the beam and flat seas. In the evening while doing about 6 knots the motion of the boat was unnoticeable. I have known more movement sitting in a marina.

Ghosting along with me up the mast sorting out the worn blocks

Saturday 6th February. Never have we experienced such constant weather, with trade winds from the North-East day after day for the past 1,000 miles, never exceeding 20 knots. The Indian Ocean, which can be the most formidable, was certainly being kind to us but with still at least another 3 days at sea there is still time to get shaken up yet. Through the day and night, we surged ahead on the rolling swell. Tonight is a full moon that lights up the ocean like a huge cauldron of mercury from its bright silver glow. It gives enough light to read comfortably. On good nights at sea, night watches can be heaven, locked away with your thoughts and the whole universe stretched out above from horizon to horizon. Only people who have spent long periods at sea can begin to understand the feeling of being part of nature. Always controlled by its awesome power, sometimes kind and gentle, sometimes ruthless and vicious, no matter how much the meteorologists claim to explain the reasons for one weather pattern or another or the reason why the barometer goes up or down, I don't think it can ever be fully understood and certainly never controlled. It seems to me a living, breathing thing with a mind of its own, that can demand respect at a whim. However over the last week or so it has certainly been in a sombre contented mood and gently pushed us across this great ocean in relative comfort.

Sunday 7th February. The wind has freshened up to about 20 knots and the sea is starting to build a little. There is about a two-meter swell coming from the North. Still making good progress though.

Monday 8th February. From the previous paragraphs I certainly ended up with egg on my face and last night was one of our worst nights at sea for a long time. Only a couple of days ago I had the feeling that the trip was not over yet. Sure enough we caught it with 35-40 knots of wind throughout the night and big breaking seas all around. With great effort I managed to hank on the storm sail, with waves thundering across the deck, to try and bring the boat speed down to a manageable pace, thereby making the motion slightly better but it was still so violent that the only safe place to sleep was on the floor of the cabin, for whoever was off watch. The wind came forward of the beam and I couldn't afford to run off too much otherwise it would have meant another five days at sea and going straight to Aden. So, we chose to push on into it. The bows of the boat seemed to burst through the tops of the oncoming breaking waves and then plummet into deep troughs and stop dead with a crash. This is the second time during our circumnavigation that we have run headlong into gales with no warning from the weather fax print outs. Only the following day did it warn of gales in the area. Most of our printouts you get reads more like a newspaper rather than a prediction.

For 24 hours we bashed our way through the seas jarring everything on the boat including ourselves. Coming off the tops of waves was a little like jumping on skis. For a moment or two the boat was in suspended animation, floating on air, then suddenly crash, you landed.

In the morning, our morale was pretty low. Everything we touched was wet or damp. Sadie rustled us up some breakfast, with superhuman effort, raising our spirits somewhat. The sun appeared from behind the clouds to dry us out and by midday we were back to usual and no longer feeling sorry for ourselves.

Another repair job

Oman

On the 13th day we sighted the coast of Oman an hour after dark. We tentatively crept into the harbour of Mina Raysut that serves as port to Salalah. I made contact by radio first and was politely directed to an anchorage within the shelter of the harbour breakwater. The next morning we were boarded by about eight officials who were very polite and offered any assistance we needed. They did put our booze into a bond until we left though.

The Chief of Police was the perfect gentleman when he came on board for diner.

Having heard so much talk of the problems in the Middle East, by the media, it was not without trepidation that we entered our first Arab country.

In Oman our fears were completely unfounded as from day one everyone we met was most kind and helpful in any way they could be. The police were very firm with their rules but, provided you played by them, they were always polite and courteous. The only rule we found a bit constrictive was a 6 o'clock curfew for all visiting yachts people. During the day we were free to come and go as we pleased.

Salalah was a Naval Base that required passports every time we went in or out. Earlier in the day a driving instructor had given us a day out in his car so, as a thank-you, we invited him and his brother to dinner on our boat. Being a Naval Base we had to get permission from the Chief of Police who had an office there. The Chief suggested it might be better if he came along too to make sure all was well. In Arabic countries, when the Chief of Police suggests something, it is best to obey so we duly gave him an invite. He turned up impeccably dressed in a spotless white pressed Arabian outfit, with impeccable manners to match. It was obvious from the driving instructor and his brother, that they were terrified of him. We all sat around the table, rather tensely at first, but after a good meal the ice broke a little. The next day when we approached the guards on the port gate, instead of taking our papers and looking at us with suspicion, they jumped to attention and saluted us through. Obviously the Chief of Police had a way of thanking us for the meal, plus the 6 o'clock curfew no longer applied to us.

A very old Arab Dhow that was stitched together with hemp string. Not a single nail or screw to be seen.

On our journey around the world each country appears to be dominated by a particular animal. For instance throughout the Pacific Islands pigs seem to have found their niche, Australia it's the Kangaroos, dogs in Bali, elephants in Sri Lanka and here its camels. Most have one thing in common, they have all learned to live, not only with man, but with traffic. The ones that have survived seem to have developed excellent sense of traffic evasion. Maybe it's just another form of evolution as the survivors keep interbreeding and slowly they develop another sense of survival. The camels here seem unperturbed by vehicles and intermingle with them happily, wandering freely in great hurts across desert or built up areas with an equal disregard.

Vicky had to dress in suitable local style clothes to walk through town to Oman.

137

We intended staying only three or four days but ended up staying for ten days with little time wasted. Our trips into the Jalala Mountains were a delight after the hot desert sun. The fresh cool air that breezed across the top of mountains encouraged one to take deep breaths and bathe in their lightly scented coolness..

Trips to the market place became a ritual for the girls browsing through the old gun market or wandering among the many perfume stalls with the scent of frankincense and musk. In other places the smell of leather in the air and the vegetable market, with all types of fresh produce brought in every morning. Oman is a very wealthy country so most Omanus can afford the best and go to great lengths to get it with anything they buy.

Aden

It was with a tinge of sadness when we slipped quietly out of Mina Rasut, bound for Aden, nearly 600 miles along the South Yemen coast. Proceeding alongside the arid sandy coloured mountains, in mirror calm conditions, it was a great temptation to pull into one of the many bays and have a dip. But to risk it we dared not, so motor on it was to be. Our routine was broken only by the landing of a 15lb Dorado always a welcome addition to our diet.

At the age of six, James could steer a course as good as anyone.

The following days saw us under spinnaker making 3-4 knots and burning the diesel at night. Since leaving Oman we had never been out of sight of the Yacht "Emerald Rose" - a 53ft Ketch from the USA. Its good to have company at sea and it also helps with the lookout for ships. Whenever one of us spotted a ship we would always give the other a call making sure it was sighted.

Day after day we motored along on a mirror calm sea with the occasional fish breaking the surface. One strange sight we saw was shoals of little red crabs, paddling along the surface by the million, apparently going nowhere. On closer inspection I noticed, while hanging my head over the side, that as the boat went near them, they span round to face us and raised their two pincers in a threatening manner until the boat had passed and then resumed their paddling. Obviously when it came to a fight, size held no fear for them. In comparison it was like us attempting to spar with King Kong.

At night the water was aglow with phosphorescence that left a trail of sparkles alongside the boat and a tube of blue light from the thrust of the propellor for about thirty yards behind the boat. With all the motoring we are having to do, I keep a regular check on the engine fluids etc. and yesterday I noticed water pouring from the front of the raw water pump on the engine. I just hope that it holds out until we reach Aden otherwise we could be out here for a considerable time. With talk on the radio of calms in just about the whole of the North Indian Ocean. Our fifth night at sea and still no wind. In the upper reaches of the Red Sea calms would be welcome, because it only blows from the North, but here it would have been nice to save diesel and rest the engine. The pattern that seems to have emerged along the coast is four hours sailing in the afternoon and motoring the other twenty hours of the day.

After six days we eventually entered the Port of Aden. Unfortunately only two weeks before they had suffered torrential rain that caused a landslide into the town and killed twenty-eight people. The town was left with a coating of dried mud over the entire area adding to an already dirty town. We decided to call in and out as quickly as possible. One thing that surprised us was the availability of most things we needed in view of the chaos there. A disturbing thing we came across was the sale of international aid goods in some of the bigger shops.

Anyhow I managed to repair our leaky water pump and fill up with diesel. That alone entailed the visiting of five different offices at the bunkering company in order to comply with all the regulations. The filling dock was awash with muddy diesel that found its way onto and into everything including the harbour water. All the yachts and dinghies were covered in black oil along the top sides, about a foot above the water line where the wash from the tug boats had washed along the sides of the boats leaving behind its black treacle. Warps and dinghy painters quickly became impregnated with the black oil. The one thing Aden had going for it was the friendliness of it's people despite the dreadful conditions and sad history over the past few years.

After a few days we did the last of our chores and fulfilled our obligations with the authorities. Our first priority was to have a general clean up and we found a suitable little island called Jahal Aziz, about twenty miles West of Aden. Ideal for the job. With paraffin and Jiff we set to work on removing the remains of Aden harbour from the boat.

The Gateway to Hell

After a good night's rest we set off for the notorious Red Sea. The straits at the southern end of the entrance are called the Straits of Bab al Mandab - translated into English reads "The Gateway to Hell". Sure enough it lived up to its reputation. On our second day out we had 40 knot winds increasing up to 50 knots the following day as the trades funnelled between the two land masses from the South as far as the Sudanese border. From there on we had head winds to look forward to. Great combers started to pile up behind us as we surfed along sometimes touching ten knots on their seething crests, with only a tiny bit of head sail flying.

As I write, I am braced at the chart table, in the middle of the night, listening to the wind screaming in the rigging. About every three or four minutes a huge breaker will choose to crash around us, with a noise like thunder, as it hammers against the sides of the boat. Its times like this you start to think of all the strains and stresses on a yacht as the sea remorselessly twists, tugs and bashes at the hull. When wind tears at the rigging you can only hope the designers and the builders have got it right.

The following morning saw us in glorious sunshine but still the howling wind tearing off the tops of the waves. Two anchorages that we considered going to we bypassed, as to make use of the southerly wind and as they both looked risky to enter in these seas and the amount of shelter they would afford us was questionable. We decided to cross over to the western side and head for Harmel Island where good shelter was reported. We didn't feel too keen on another night at sea in these conditions but there are times when the elements and anchorages force you to press on against your will. There is nothing we would like more than to put our feet up and have a good night's rest.

When a group of yachts have experienced a gale together there are always a few interesting stories to follow. One such story, aboard the 53ft yacht "Emerald Rose", was that during the gale they suffered a knock down. Howard was on watch and Sharon his wife was asleep on the port berth. Howard hung on for his life and when the boat righted itself Sharon awoke on the starboard berth wondering what the commotion was all out. Even though the boat is 15ft wide Sharon never suffered a single scratch. Our friends Keith and Carol off "Kirsten Jayne" had a similar knock down. Unfortunately they were not quite so lucky. They had their dinghy torn from their davits and the tv smashed as it flew across the cabin. Fortunately Keith managed to retrieve the dinghy, which was no mean feat in such a sea. Boats throughout the area were reporting similar problems. The main complaint was losing odds and ends overboard, including gas bottles, buckets etc. One boat had his binoculars washed away out of his cockpit.

Eventually after three days of wild toboggan rides the wind and sea went to sleep again. By six in the morning we were off the island of Harmel. Harmel is part of Eritrea, which has been fighting a long and bloody war with Ethiopia to gain independence. We are not officially supposed to be here but as the tiny island is 60 miles offshore and uninhabited we figure we'll be left in peace. Having had three consecutive nights without any real sleep we are willing to take the chance. The following day we can push on to the Sudanease border 150 miles to the North. After a walk on the flat sandy island, whose only inhabitants seem to be Hermit crabs, we spent a blissful night's sleep in the flat calm anchorage.

On our exit from the bay we were alarmed to see numerous isolated coral heads which we had to snake around with Sadie, on the end of the bow spirit, shouting directions. Once in open water the sailing was delightful with steady south-easterly winds wafting us along at 5 knots on the flat blue seas. I tossed the fishing line over the side and no sooner had the slack taken up, a 20lb fish struck. We never did determine the species but it looked a little like a Queen fish. However, the fish possessed a beautiful white meat to rival any fish we caught so far.

During the afternoon the wind picked up a little giving good speed until our rotten old spinnaker gave way almost tearing in half but for the two thin strips down each edge. Tomorrow the sewing machine will be out again. The poor old sail will soon be more patches than original spinnaker, but it does pull well in light airs due to sheer size and owes us nothing. In New Zealand I asked the sail maker in Gulf Harbour to service it for me. When he looked at it he started laughing because he thought I was playing a joke on him. He didn't believe it could still be used but 15,000 miles later I'm still using it and still patching it!! I no longer bother what colour the patches are so you can imagine how it looks. I wonder how much longer I can keep it going? Having lost our spinnaker temporarily, it was as though the wind obliged by freshening so that we no longer need it for the time being.

Through the night we surged on at good speed in flat seas. However, all good things come to an end, and on the VHF radio early in the morning we heard the weather was on the change, with 35 knots predicted from the North West. A quick decision was reached to head for shelter behind a tiny island with a big name "Tallatallasaghir" where hopefully there would be a safe refuge. At least the wind had held good to get us past the notorious Ethiopian coast from where it is not unheard of for yachts to be used as target practice.

The incredible ancient town of Suakin, now sadly little more than ruins.

Having reached Tallatallasaghir we were disappointed to find the anchorage untenable due to a heavy swell rolling in from the South East. So a decision was made to head for Trinkitat - a bay on the mainland of Sudan. Being mid-afternoon we were limited for time and couldn't afford to get it wrong. To be in an area of concentrated reefs, with 35 knots predicted, is not recommended. As relatively few yachts cruise this area, scant information is available so you are dependent to a greater degree on your own judgement as to whether or not the spot you pick to drop your hook is going to be comfortable.

Trinkitat was a reasonable anchorage though very desolate. On our venture ashore we were greeted by the gruesome sight of a dead camel lying in the parched desert. The place had a lonely, eerie feel to it that made us want to get out as soon as possible.

The only snag we now faced was the maze of reefs to wind our way through to get to Suakin. As it turned out it looked far more formidable on the chart than in practice as the reef stood out well in good light. To our surprise there were more beacons than the chart showed through the narrow channels.

The sad poverty stricken town of Suakin.

Having reached the town of Suakin we made first contact with the Sudanese authorities who welcomed us into their bureaucratic net. Again here, as in many third world countries, nothing can be done without reams of paperwork that requires queuing for long periods of time.

Having completed the ritual we were allowed ashore for three hours to do our shopping and sight-seeing. Wanting to see a little more you had to go through the whole procedure again the next day for a second three-hour shore leave. The whole affair was well worth the effort though as Suakin is still a trading centre where large camel trains arrive from the desert carrying Bedouin tribesmen to the incredibly poor town. To walk around the place is like stepping back two thousand years. But Suakin couldn't have always been poor. Some of the building, though falling down into crumbling piles of rock, still bear evidence of the bygone era of splendour and wealth.

Indeed the old city is now deserted but it was obviously a beautiful place in its time. Built on an island, bridged by a causeway, the old city is separate from the now functional town.

A typically dressed local.   *A proud Nomad of the desert.*

Walking through the ruins gave one an eerie feeling as great eagles soared above like vultures waiting for a meal from the dry parched landscape. Shapes and shadows from the relics gave the place a feeling of unreality, almost as if everything had been placed there for a horror movie. In the new town (only 1,000-years-old) few motorised vehicles could be seen, as in this part of the world the principal transport is still the camel, followed by a close second, the donkey. It was strange to see scores of camels parked as we would park cars at a parking lot at home, all patiently waiting the return of their masters. We managed to procure a few vegetables to replenish our dwindling stores, but it wasn't quite as easy as it sounds. Everywhere we moved we were followed by hordes of children all eager to try out their few words of English on us that they had learned at school. "How are you mister?" was the phrase that echoed around us all the time. So far the vast majority of Arabs we have met have been honest and trustworthy to be honest with us and great honour seems to be instilled in them to this aim. I believe that things will be very different when we reach Egypt though, but here we felt we struck fair bargains.

On the 14th March we made an early start out of the old slave trading city to start once again on our way north against the seemingly ever present northerly winds. Fortunately nature has provided for the north bound boats with very convenient gaps in the reef, or Marsas as they are called, that allow a yacht to play musical chairs with the wind.

The Red Sea has areas that rarely see any people for months on end.

They give good protection when the wind blows hard. The Marsas seem strategically placed about every 10-15 miles apart, on average. Without them life would be extremely tough for Northbound yachts. The other advantage, that is well worth a mention, is the marvellous living on the reefs around the Marsas. We found most of the dives superior to the Great Barrier Reef, insomuch as the water had much better clarity. Maybe that was due to the respective times we were in the different areas though. Any keen diver could not help being impressed by the fabulous underwater gardens of every colour imaginable, patrolled by myriads of fish wearing gaudy suits of all shapes and sizes. It came as little surprise to learn that Jacques Cousteau chose this area to set an underwater observatory. In one dive alone we must have witnessed at least 500 different varieties of fish.

Our life aboard fell into a daily routine of 6 a.m start, with anchor down again by early afternoon. To try to enter reef anchorages later in the day is a dangerous business. While the sun is overhead, or behind you, the reefs stand out pretty well. Once the sun goes ahead of you the reflection on the water makes them virtually invisible. The only way to navigate through inlets is by eyeball. The other thing that needs to be considered is that many areas of the Red Sea are poorly charted. It is not uncommon to see a tell-tale patch of water where a reef or 'bommie' as they are called, looms just below the surface, but has no mention on the chart. The Red Sea is renowned for strong northerly winds in the northern sector and, over the next few days, it was to show us just what it could do. We struggled on gaining 10-25 miles a day on the short choppy seas that had the knack of stopping any small boat dead in its tracks.

On reaching Taila Islands we eventually ground to a halt as the head winds stiffened up to a solid 30 knots and continued to do so for the next four days. It held us trapped in our own little world, tucked in behind a tiny sand spit with nothing more to do but hang on and wait.

As always, eventually the slight easing of the wind we had been waiting for came and on we pushed. While passing between the mainland and Muchawar Island we experienced a rather frightening episode that won't easily be forgotten. Whilst under full sail we could see a tiny boat in the distance coming our way. We thought nothing more of it as it is not unusual to have small fishing boats come alongside asking for cigarettes and fishing hooks etc. On this occasion things were a little different. As the boat approached, with three men on board, to my horror I saw one-man crouch down behind a machine gun mounted on a tripod in the front on the boat. He then proceeded to load it with a belt of bullets fed from a box. He pointed it straight at us while another man signalled us to stop. We had no choice but to obey and round up to windward. I'm sure they could, and would, have riddled us with bullets had we not complied. Three rough looking men clambered aboard armed with machine guns and asked to see our papers but, before I had chance to show him, he was demanding whiskey. I lied to him saying I didn't have any so then another asked for beer. Thinking this the easiest way out of the situation I surrendered my beer reluctantly.

It is not a nice feeling being surrounded by men with automatic machine guns in their hands but my heart went into my mouth as James emerged from below with his black plastic bow and arrow with a red rubber sucker on the end and shot one of the men. Fortunately, they saw the funny side of it and all burst into uncontrollable laughter, thereby defusing a very tense situation. After a short conflab between themselves they decided to leave us alone, much to our relief.

Flat calm tucked in behind one of the numerous reefs that served us so well.

Throughout the third world yachties seem to be a target for free cigarettes, booze and occasionally food. This is the first time however that we were not given the option to say "no". It is difficult to refuse someone something when you are looking down the barrel of a gun.

To have antagonised these people would have been a very foolhardy and dangerous thing to do. They claim they were officials but in truth they were nothing more than small-time pirates, with no papers, uniforms or identification - the only authority was the machine guns they carried.

Feeling relieved to be away we pushed north anchoring in all types of places. One place of shelter was behind the wreck of a big ship. Often, we would anchor behind reefs with no land in sight. That always seemed somewhat strange as the boat appeared to be in the open ocean at anchor but the reefs do provide efficient shelter from the swell.

At the last stop in Sudan we had quite a surprise when a total of seven boats shared the remote Marsa Umbeila for the night. In the evening a barbecue was organised with a whole desert as a beach to build a fire on.

In these areas a strange phenomenon occurs whenever you step ashore. Even though no houses or huts can be seen for miles, or indeed anything to sustain life, nothing more than sand and more sand, people seem to appear as if by magic from nowhere. What they live on is a complete mystery as nothing can grow on the land. The sea abounds with fish but you never see any fishing boats in the remote areas or anyone fishing.

That night at the barbecue a Nomad appeared out of thin air and sat about 50 yards from us. We took him some food for which he smiled and nodded, ate it and disappeared just as quick as he came. A couple of hours later another Nomad told us through hand signals that he wanted some water, after which he tramped off into the hot desert bound for heaven knows where. He was dressed in a heavy overcoat with his sword hanging at his side. Within minutes he was out of sight.

Most of the Nomads carry either a sword or a large curved knife (some have both), which they take great pride in and keep them razor sharp. A good sword is handed down from generation to generation with consecutive owners often adding a little decorative art to the handle or scabbard. Consequently many of the swords are of great age and very decorative. It's not uncommon for them to be in excess of 300 years old according to a local doctor who befriended us in Suakin. When I enquired as to the value of them word soon got around and the next day I was greeted with several people wanting to sell me a sword. In the end I was talked into purchasing one that liked the look of, mainly for its ornate properties.

On returning to the boat our doctor friend turned up to see us again. My sword had an Arabic inscription on the blade, which I asked him to translate for me. On inspection he looked rather embarrassed as he revealed that the sword had been used to fight against the British many years ago and the inscription was asking God to protect the user. Our friend was surprised to see that I was delighted to have found one with such a history. He thought it an insult to be offered the purchase of a sword that had been used against our own people.

We finally departed Sudan and crossed the invisible line into Egypt. With a fair forecast we motor-sailed for the next two days and nights of the relatively calm spell and made up some ground towards Suez.

The Red Sea is a test for the entire boat and crew as in the southern part there are very strong southerly winds and in the North, strong northerlies almost constantly during this time of year. For this reason a very short steep chop builds up and stops the boat dead on every wave. It required the use of engine more than anywhere else during our whole circumnavigation to make head-way. From the sailor's point a constant careful watch is necessary due to the number of ships in the middle. If one keeps nearer to the shore the numerous reefs then become another problem.

The whole affair we found very tiring and stressful because if something goes wrong up this stretch of water it is a major problem. There are only one or two possible places to get any repairs done during the whole length of the Red Sea. Towns are almost non-existent and, when a town is found, supplies of any sort are a rarity. So all in all you are on your own from the time you enter the Red Sea for the next 1,000 miles of often painfully slow progress. All you can do is hope that everything keeps working, both fitness wise with the crew and mechanically with the boat.

A mini cruise to the Pyamids

We made use of every calm spell until we reached Safaga, where we left the boat for four days after enrolling into the mind-boggling net of Egyptian bureaucracy. In Egypt every opportunity of checking your papers and passport is taken by anyone remotely connected with the army, police, immigration, customs etc, just in the hope of gathering "baksheesh" from you. Baksheesh incidentally is the Egyptian term for 'tip', be it in the form of cigarettes, beer, clothes, money or anything else they can get from you.

The gigantic statues of Luxor

After filling in a multitude of forms and with the local bureaucrats pacified for a while we negotiated with a mini bus owner to visit the ancient town of Luxor where the Valley of the Kings and the Great Karnak Temple is situated, on the banks of the Nile. After two hours of driving through dry mountains and arid desert the distinct line of green finally arrived. This is where the life blood of the country starts to irrigate the land turning the dry desert into lush verdant countryside. Crops of all types spread as far as the eye can see where only a few minutes before only sand could be seen.

Luxor is a bustling city that once was the administrative centre of Egypt during the reign of the Pharaohs. Each Pharaoh left behind a succession of legacies in the form of great temples, designed and built to last forever. The size of some of the temples is awe inspiring and nowhere is it demonstrated better than at Karnak, the home of Amun, the creator God of Egypt. The giant hyper-style halls with towering columns would be a challenge to any builder even today using all the modern technology. Probably one of the greatest of hyper-style halls was the one built during Ramses 2 reign with 136 columns of monstrous proportions. Enough history and back to the present.

Ancient Fellucas on the Nile make a remarkable effective way of travel.

No visit to Egypt is complete without a trip on the Nile. The only way to do this is to sail on one of the ancient Feluccas that still ply up and down the Nile today as they did 1,000 years ago. The Feluccas drift effortlessly along gathering every wisp of breeze with their towering lateen rigs that handle so easily. Somehow it seemed so much more fitting to drift along under sail in this ancient land than to roar along on one of the modern cruisers that so much resemble floating blocks of flats. Aboard the little Felucca we gently sailed along as the magnificent ball of red fire gradually dropped below the horizon of the Valley of the Kings to close yet another day in Egypt.

After three nights in Luxor we were eager to get back to Gringo to make sure all was well after our excursion. As we entered the little town of Safaga we could see our boat swinging at anchor in the sheltered bay where we left her waiting for us. We always get the feeling of home-coming on our return after we have left the boat for a while. I am sure that every sailor develops an affection for their boats especially when they have travelled long distances and learned their every creak and groan. We are no exception.

The next day we motor-sailed north into the almost perpetual northerly winds towards Hurghada and the Gulf of Suez. Hurghada is a famous diving area but, having been spoilt by diving in places like Bonaire, the Pacific and further south in the Red Sea we felt a little disappointed. The water was too cold and the coral no more spectacular than dozens of other places we have dived in.

Talking of spectacular sights, a couple of nights later saw us sailing up the Gulf of Suez during the night, with its multitude of oil wells all burning off their excess gas. The sky was ablaze with the orange glow of the oversized torches that formed a gauntlet for ships and yachts to sail between. It was a real test of concentration to weave a yacht through all the rigs, ships and fishing boats during a night passage- definitely not for the faint-hearted. We survived the gauntlet to arrive in the Port of Suez in absolute mirror calm conditions with more than a slight feeling of relief when we tied up outside the yacht club. Like all experiences in life it never seems quite so bad when you can put your feet up, relax and contemplate the events gone by. After a day at Suez spent washing red dust from the rigging and decks we planned a trip to Cairo and the Pyramids of Giza.

At 7 a.m we clambered aboard a local bus with kids and kit in tow and paid our £4 Egyptian (approx. 0.80p). Had we gone through an agent it would have cost about $50. Arriving in Cairo we got caught in something we did not expect, a heat wave!! The temperature soared to an incredible 43 degrees with not a breath of air, leaving us, and even the locals, panting for breath. We stayed a couple of days in Cairo. Fortunately on the second day the temperature, though still hot, dropped a little. We proceeded to do the usual touristy things of camel riding around the Pyramids and visiting the well-trodden circuit of sites, seemingly all laid on for the visitor. One experience that will stay with us was the Cairo Museum with its treasures from the ancient Pharaoh of Egypt. The finest exhibit was the exquisite golden face mask of Tutankhamen. It is bewildering to think that the Egyptians were building magnificent constructions and producing incredible works of art when most of the rest of the world were living in caves. Surely with the level of craftsmanship and artistic flair it could not have all been produced by slaves. Sadly Egypt has gone from the highest standard of building the world has ever seen to probably one of the lowest. Where has all the great knowledge and skill gone?

The only way to see the Pyramids is from the back of a camel, but be prepared for some haggling

Today Egypt is sadly bogged down with bureaucracy and corruption. On entering Egypt the first eight money transactions we did we were short changed on every single one including a bank withdrawal!! Fortunately we had prior warning and were on guard ready for it. Nothing gets done here without backsheesh being paid from the very bottom to the top. In order to get a yacht through the Suez Canal the following offices all have to be pacified.

1.   Suez Canal tonnage certificate.
2.   Customs clearance.
3.   Transit Fees.
4.   Insurance

5. Port and light fees
6. Pilot fees
7. Security clearance
8. Coast Guard authorities.
9. Currency transfer receipts
10. Passports
11. Six copies of crew lists
12. Health certificates.
13. Security permit.
14. Customs list of yacht equipment.

The only way around all this is to pay an agent around $200 which was the going rate when we transited. I would imagine little of that would be left after the agent had greased all the official palms.

Arrest in Suez Canal

The trip through the canal is split into two transits, with an overnight stop at Ismailia. We could not complain about either of the pilots, especially our first who was enthusiastic and very good at his job. All went according to plan for the first half although we were asked for gifts at Ismailia when a boat came to pick up our Pilot. The second part of the trip started off smoothly enough but again 'presents' were asked for by the delivery boat crew when our Pilot arrived.

The trouble really started on reaching Port Said where Police boats and Pilot boats acted like a pack of hungry wolves trying to squeeze the last bit of baksheesh out of all the yachts just before they leave Egypt. We were boarded by the police from their boat and immediately asked for cigarettes. No sooner had they left, a pilot boat barges alongside. I was at the wheel of our boat trying to avoid damage whilst Sadie and the children were busy with fenders to hold them off. The crew of the pilot boat boarded us like Pirates moving in for the kill. At this I blew my top and physically started pushing them back to where they had come, with lots of shouting and hollering at each other. We managed to escape but as we pulled away we realised that we still had one of them on board. We continued for the exit hoping to drop him off at the nearest convenient point but we were then headed off by a canal work boat who forced us to head off to Port Said Marina. Then great confusion ensued with raised voices and arm waving and everyone trying to give their side of the story at the same time. The police then arrived and started to take statements. By this time the whole incident was getting out of hand. I had real horrible thoughts of spending the night in an Egyptian prison. Then like an angel out of the blue, the manager of the yacht club arrived who well knew the crux of the problem and managed to pour oil over troubled waters. The truth was they all knew what the problem was but none would admit to intimidating yachts into handing over baksheesh. In the end I had to bite my lip and apologise to the canal pilot in order to restore his pride. I escaped without handing money over to them but whether all the hassle was worth it. I have serious doubts. In Egypt tips are not hoped for but demanded. After a couple of months here it starts to grate on the most tolerant people's nerves.

At last on our way through the Suez.

Cyprus

The following day we were glad to get to sea away from all the aggravation and bound for Cyprus, even though the wind was bang on the nose, where else would we have expected it to be? The choppy confused sea gradually adopted a more regular pattern as we approached deeper water. Gringo once more got down to the task of delivering us to our destination where we could once again clean off the red dust from her rigging and decks and all the scruff and tyre marks off her topsides. The calling cards of all visitors in the Suez Canal.

The second night out saw us 30 miles south of Cyprus working our way through the busy shipping lanes to the Port of Larnaca, still hard on the wind as we had been since Sudan. For some reason sailing to windward always seems to wear us down quicker than sailing off the wind, due to the heeling and motion. After only two nights at sea we were both feeling tired and ready for a good night's rest. We felt something we had not experienced for about three years as we closed the coast - cold rain. At least it helped to wash away some of the fine sand dust deposited in our rigging from the deserts along the Red Sea.

After a few weeks well-earned rest in Cyrpus, we hauled Gringo out for an anti-foul. It was then we were approached by someone who wanted to buy Gringo. At first I refused to sell, but then common sense took over and I agreed to deliver her across the Med. Partly to help the buyer and partly so we could complete our circumnavigation. During the three years of sailing we had accumulated all sorts of mementos from around the world. I was pondering the thought of how to get them all home, when I discovered an old 1963 Falmouth Pilot 31ft in the corner of the marina for sale. On inspection it was obviously neglected, but seemed solidly built being pitch pine on oak frames. To cut a long story short I purchased the boat where she lay for £2,000. We cleaned and painted her before loading all the things we treasure to take home.

We still had to deliver Gringo, so we were soon on our way again bound for Castillo Horizon 300 miles to the West. A Greek Island lying within spitting distance from the mainland of Turkey. We sailed up through the Aegean Islands, our destination being Athens where the new owners awaited her arrival. With mixed feelings, one being a slight anti-climax at the thought of it all being over. Another line of thought was excitement at the idea of seeing all our family and friends in the not too distant future that we had not seen for so long.

Our next plan was then to go back to Cyprus that year and sail

"Modeste" back to Guernsey. Unfortunately by the time we got to Athens it was too late in the season and I needed to get back home to sort out my business. We had not been home for three years.

On arrival in Cyprus we had the feeling that our trip was almost over.

I would have liked to have spent more time in many of the places we had visited. I feel that three years was not really long enough to sail around the world. Maybe five years would be a more reasonable time to complete the trip. During the complete circumnavigation, I would estimate ten percent of the time has been a little frustrating, often arising from the entanglement of bureaucracy, and a small percentage of hardship arising from adverse weather. Having said this, I believe that all of us thoroughly enjoyed the experience, with memories to last a life time. We set out to take it easy, not attempting to break any records, and I think for the average family sailor, that is the best way to go about it. The only record we can lay claim to, is being the first Guernsey family to fly the Guernsey flag around the world as far as we know. The most important thing we have gained is knowledge of people, places and sailing in that order. The things that we will miss most are probably the intimacy with the boat and family. Every squeak and groan from the old boat was as if she was talking to us. Letting us know if she was over pressed, or not happily balanced. Almost automatically Sadie or myself would ease a sheet or tweak the course a little when necessary. In a choppy sea, on a pitch-dark night, we could lay our hands straight onto a hand hold, and duck our head at the right moment to avoid a crack on the skull. If we attended a sailing school for the rest of our lives, I don't think we could ever get attuned to a boat so closely again. A person who is plunged into a situation where he has no one else to turn to for help quickly learns how to cope, if he has a reasonably inquisitive mind. When life can depend on that skill, it is amazing how quickly the knowledge is homed. It's probably all part of our instinct for survival.

Anyway, we left our new acquisition "Modeste" in Cyprus until the following season. I went back with an old friend of mine Robin Swift as Sadie was not interested in sailing "an old boat" back, plus the children has settled into a schooling routine. That in itself was quite an epic voyage, but little Modeste performed pretty well and safely got us across the Med. In the meantime, unbeknown to me or Robin, Sadie advertised Modeste in a classic boat magazine and we landed up trading it for a farmhouse in France!!

We did keep the farmhouse for four years, but you never loose the sailing bug. Since then we have had a succession of boats. I bought a Bruce Robert 45' in Stavanger, Norway. We sailed her through the Caledonian Canal, across to Ireland and then back to Guernsey. After selling "Nordic Warrior" I then bought a Triton 48 from an auction in Rhodos. We sailed "Crystal" from Rhodos across the Aegean to the Ionian and sailed extensively around that area including Croatia. Not long after "Crystal" I purchased a Moody 54 "Graceful" in Scotland and sailed her down to the Greek Isles. As luck would have it, an Italian Gentleman fell in love with her, so we sold it to him.

Now we are sailing a Moody 47 often with our friends Tom and Sherida from "Distant Song" who also have another boat (we had Christmas diner with them all those years ago in Thailand). We have cruised the Med extensively for many years now. We do not have any plans of doing anymore long distant cruising. We don't have the stamina anymore.

As for our children, twenty nine years on they are both happily married. Vicky is a qualified Chartered Surveyor and has been elected as a politician for the States of Guernsey. James is running his own business and is a qualified Tree Surgeon. All that climbing up the mast must have sown a seed.

Acknowlegements

A special big thank you to my long suffering wife Sadie who over the last forty years has been my right hand man and backed me in anything I undertook. She persevered for many hours typing this book from my handwritten scribble. There is no one earth I would rather have done this trip with.

Thank you also to Andrea Bunce, Deputy Richard Graham, Nick Bennet and Peter Dawson-Ball for proof-reading my book. I know how busy all your lives are. Your time and expertise was greatly appreciated.

Our daughter Vicky. Originally my book was written on an old typewriter. Computers were not invented then. Thank you for converting and retyping parts of my story to a computer. I know how frustrating that was.

Kathleen Meeks. Over dinner you helped us choose the title.

Denis Wilkins

I was born in Bilston the West Midlands in 1949. I became hooked on anything that floated from an early age. When my friends at sixteen went and bought motorbikes, I bought a little boat, built a cabin on it and set off from the Midlands to Llangothlin, North Wales.

I was self taught in almost everything I undertook, eventually becoming a very successful businessman, now retired in Guernsey, still looking for more adventures.